Hernando Cortés

THE WORLD'S GREAT EXPLORERS

Hernando Cortés

By R. Conrad Stein

Consultant: Robert Somerlott,
Lecturer in Mexican History,
Instituto Allende of the
University of Guanajuato, Mexico

CHILDRENS PRESS ®
CHICAGO

This page:
Cortés's conquest of Mexico

Opposite page: Mural depicting the different castes, or social classes, in Aztec society

Project Editor: Ann Heinrichs
Designer: Lindaanne Donohoe
Cover Art: Steven Gaston Dobson
Engraver: Liberty Photoengraving

**Library of Congress
Cataloging-in Publication Data**

Stein, R. Conrad.
  Hernando Cortés / by R. Conrad Stein.

    p.   cm. — (The World's great explorers)
    Includes bibliographical references (p.124]
and index.
    Summary: A biography of Mexico's con-
queror.
    ISBN 0-516-03059-0

    1. Cortés, Hernán, 1485-1547—Juvenile
literature. 2. Conquerors—Mexico—Biogra-
phy—Juvenile literature. 3. Governors—
Mexico—Biography—Juvenile literature. 4.
Mexico—History—Conquest, 1519-1540 [1.
Cortés, Hernando, 1485-1547. 2. Explorers. 3.
Mexico—History—Conquest, 1519-1540-]
I. Title. II. Series.
F1230.C835S74   1991
972'.02'092—dc20
[B]   90-20655
[92]   CIP
                                       AC

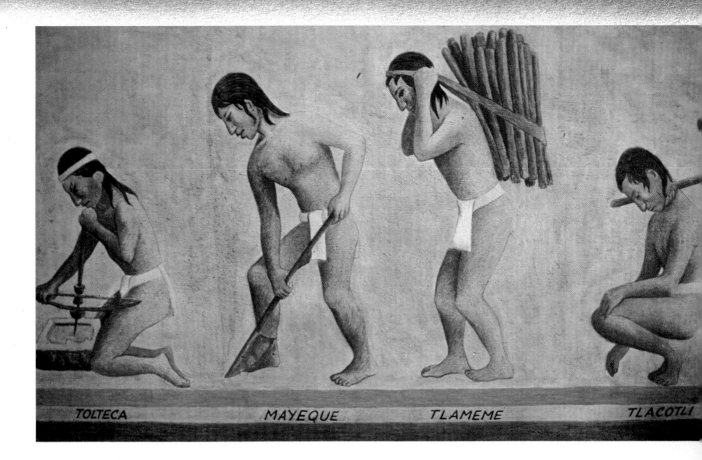

TOLTECA   MAYEQUE   TLAMEME   TLACOTLI

Table of Contents

Chapter 1
The Enchanting Valley

Dawn. November 8, 1519.

Below the Spaniards spread the Valley of Mexico, where marvelous cities rose from the shore of a great glistening lake. As they marched closer, the Spaniards noted that even the humblest houses of the cities were plastered with lime and gleamed in the sun as if the walls were made of silver.

Soon the Spaniards arrived at the outskirts of Tenochtitlán, ancient Mexico City. Tenochtitlán was the capital of the mighty Aztec nation. The city rose from an island in the center of a lake. It was larger than any town in Spain. In fact, the Aztec capital was probably the largest city in the world at that time.

All their lives the Spanish soldiers had waited for a moment like this. They were plunderers who hungered for gold. This island city, they believed, was so rich that even its poorest citizens ate from gold plates.

An Aztec mural, now in Mexico City's Anthropology Museum

But during this moment of discovery, the soldiers were so overwhelmed with the marvels of Aztec civilization that even gold lost its luster. One of the marching soldiers was Bernal Díaz del Castillo, who years later wrote a book about the Spanish expedition to Mexico. He described the Spaniards' descent into the Valley of Mexico as one might retell a visit to another planet: "And when we saw so many cities and villages . . . we were amazed and said it was like the enchantments they tell of in the legends. . . . And some of our soldiers asked whether the things we saw were not a dream."

Riding at the head of the Spanish column was their leader, Hernando Cortés. Historians would later hail him as one of the greatest explorers and military

Cortés's capture of Mexico City, an engraving from a painting by Alonzo Chappel

commanders of all time. Surely at this moment he must have pondered his military situation. He commanded four hundred foot soldiers and fifteen horsemen. He led this tiny force into the heartland of a potential enemy that could put 100,000 soldiers in the field at a moment's notice.

Despite the misgivings that must have echoed in his thoughts, Cortés rode ramrod straight. He wore his Spanish pride arrogantly, as if it were armor. His men mirrored their leader, refusing to show fear even in the teeth of danger.

Bernal Díaz later looked back on the boldness of Cortés and the Spaniards as they marched into the valley and marveled, "What men have there been in the world who have shown such daring!"

Chapter 2
Spain and the New World

> *"We came [to the New World] to serve God and the monarch—and also to get rich."*
>
> —*Bernal Díaz del Castillo*

For seven hundred years the men of Spain fought the Moors who came from North Africa and occupied most of the country. Finally, at the end of the fifteenth century, the Spaniards broke the Moors' last grip on their land. When not battling the Moors, the Spaniards fought each other as provinces within the country waged bitter civil wars. The almost constant warfare turned Spain into a military society. The nation's youth thought of war as a glorious adventure. Raw courage on the battlefield became the true test of Spanish manhood.

Caceres, a medieval city in the Extremadura region of Spain

Into this kingdom of warriors Hernando Cortés was born in 1485. He grew up in Extremadura, a province that hugs the present-day border between Spain and Portugal. Windswept and treeless, Extremadura was the poorest region in all of Spain. Perhaps because of its poverty, the province produced some of Spain's most courageous warriors. To a young Extremaduran, a military life, despite its dangers, was more alluring than trying to farm the sandy and unyielding soil.

The Cortés family was one of minor nobility. Hernando's father was a cavalry officer. His mother was a sternly religious woman from old provincial stock. Francisco López de Gómara, who was Cortés's secretary and biographer, said about the Cortés family, "They had little wealth, but much honor."

As a boy Cortés was frail and sickly. On many occasions he lay on his bed, gripped by fever and hovering near death. The family housekeeper served as his nurse and offered up prayers to St. Peter to spare the boy's life. When he became an adult, Cortés always honored the feast day of St. Peter.

At age fourteen, Cortés was sent to the university at Salamanca, where he studied Latin and law. He was probably a superior student, for later in life many learned people considered him to be a Latin scholar. But he stayed only two years at the university. Restless and brooding, he returned to his home in Extremadura. His biographer Gómara described Cortés at this stage of his life as being quarrelsome, irritable, and "a source of trouble to his parents."

While Cortés was growing up, Spain enjoyed a series of triumphs that made the country a world power. The marriage between Prince Ferdinand of

Doors of the university at Salamanca, Spain

Boabdil, the last king of the Moors, surrendering to Ferdinand and Isabella

Aragon and Princess Isabella of Castile united the Spanish provinces and brought an end to the civil wars. In 1492 Spanish forces captured Granada, the last bastion of Moorish power in the country. Also in 1492, Ferdinand and Isabella sent the Italian sea captain Christopher Columbus on a mission to find a new trade route to the East. Columbus failed to find the coveted trade route, but he planted the first seeds of the Spanish empire in the New World.

A young Hernando Cortés dreamed about crossing the Atlantic to find excitement and riches on the frontier of the Spanish empire. His parents managed to gather the money for his ship passage. In 1504, at age nineteen, Cortés sailed for the New World. He would soon join a small army of adventurers who wrote a bold but bloody chapter in world history.

Historians call the Spaniards who explored the New World and overwhelmed the native people the *conquistadores* (conquerors). They were among the boldest explorers that history has ever known. Casting aside dangers such as starvation or attack by hostile natives, they bravely plunged into unknown lands. But it was greed rather than the pure quest for discovery that aroused their interests in exploration. The *conquistadores* hoped to enrich themselves on the lands they explored and conquered. Their leaders were men like Cortés who, though they lacked money, were noble born and too proud to work. The common soldiers included former priests, ex-prisoners, farm boys hungry for excitement, and vicious cutthroats.

Gold held a special magic for the *conquistadores*. Not only would the precious metal bring comfort on earth; it was believed that, by donating gold to the church, a man might buy a place in heaven. Even before the voyage of Columbus, Spain was haunted by rumors of cities lying somewhere across the sea where gold was so plentiful it was used as roofing material. With gold as a lure, the *conquistadores* flocked to the new lands discovered by Christopher Columbus.

During his first two voyages, Columbus established a colony on an island in the West Indies that he called Hispaniola. The island today contains the nations of Haiti and the Dominican Republic. On Hispaniola lived the primitive Arawak Indians. Columbus described them as being "gentle and kind." At first they worshiped the Spaniards as if they were gods. But the Spaniards mistreated the Arawak horribly. A war broke out between the two peoples, and the Arawak were slaughtered by the Spaniards' superior weapons and military skill.

When the nineteen-year-old Hernando Cortés arrived in Hispaniola, the colony consisted of little else but the muddy frontier outpost of Santo Domingo. As a man of noble rank, he was offered a large tract of land to establish a farm. Cortés said, angrily, that he had not traveled to the New World to scratch the dirt like a peasant, but to find gold.

Nevertheless, Cortés accepted land and Indian slaves and became a prosperous sugar farmer. He satisfied his thirst for excitement by gambling and by pursuing the few Spanish women on the island.

Spanish settlements in the West Indies expanded to the nearby islands of Puerto Rico and Jamaica. Next the *conquistadores* turned their attention to the fertile lands of Cuba. A wealthy Hispaniola landowner named Diego Velázquez de Cuellar headed a four-ship, three-hundred-man expedition that touched Cuba's shores in 1511. Serving as Velázquez's secretary was the sugar planter Hernando Cortés. Although Velázquez and Cortés worked together reasonably well, neither man trusted the other.

The conquest of Cuba was another easy venture for the Spaniards. The only Indian leader who tried to organize resistance was a man named Hatuey. A native of Hispaniola, Hatuey fled that island to escape Spanish brutality. His story illustrates the Spaniards' reign of terror in the West Indies. Because he was a rebel, a Spanish court condemned Hatuey to death. Before he was to die, a Spanish priest offered to baptize Hatuey so that his soul might enter heaven. He asked the priest if there were Spaniards in this place called heaven. The priest answered yes. Hatuey declined baptism, claiming that heaven was surely not a paradise if a single Spaniard resided there.

The cruel execution of Hatuey

Hernando Cortés built a huge ranch in Cuba and raised livestock. He stayed on the island for seven years, married a woman from a Spanish family, and built one of the finest houses in the New World. Gómara said of his life-style in Cuba, "All he did, in his presence, bearing, conversation, manner of eating and dressing gave signs of his being a great lord."

Despite Cortés's wealth, his spirit remained restless. He believed that somewhere in these newly discovered lands was a vast empire for him to discover, explore, and conquer.

The Mayan temple of El Castillo at Chichén Itzá in Mexico

The Spaniards of the West Indies knew nothing of Mexico, the huge land that lay to their west. Then, in 1517, a ship commanded by the Spanish sea captain Francisco Hernandez Cordoba was blown off course and landed on the shores of Mexico's Yucatán Peninsula. What Cordoba saw on the Yucatán astonished him. Here were stone cities and natives who dressed in cotton clothes. It was the first highly developed civilization the Spaniards found in the New World.

Diego Velázquez, the recently appointed governor of Cuba, was intrigued by Cordoba's reports. Could this strange land contain the fabled cities where gold was so plentiful? Velázquez sent out an expedition to probe the Mexican coast and learned that the new land was a huge mass, not another tiny island. The Cuban governor next planned to send a large mission of Spaniards to explore this inviting land and search for riches. To command the exploration party, the governor chose Hernando Cortés. It was a choice Velázquez soon regretted.

With great energy, Cortés began making ready for the voyage. A new world beckoned, and finally he felt on the threshold of fulfilling his destiny. At the time, Cortés had lived in the West Indies for fourteen years. Though he had grown wealthy, he still lacked the fame he so desperately sought. Now he looked west across the sea, where lands never before seen by Europeans lay waiting for him alone to master.

Governor Velázquez soon had second thoughts about Cortés. The man's entire personality seemed to change as he prepared for his mission. This ambitious commander, Velázquez believed, intended to organize his own empire in the new lands and become more powerful even than the governor of Cuba.

Diego Velázquez de Cuellar, who commissioned Cortés's expedition

Giving in to his many fears, Velázquez wrote an order withdrawing Cortés's permission to sail. But Cortés's spies warned him that the governor was about to change his mind. Heeding the warnings, Cortés boarded a ship off Cuba's coast. Under Spanish law, the written order relieving him of his assignment had to be delivered in person. As long as Cortés avoided agents of Velázquez, he could keep his command. For three months, Cortés remained on shipboard off the coast of Cuba while he gathered his army. A frustrated Velázquez, meanwhile, vowed he would some-day punish this insolent upstart.

In February 1519, Cortés's preparations were complete. Sailing on board eleven ships, the Cortés expedition left the Cuban shore bound for the Yucatán

Pedro de Alvarado

Peninsula. His force consisted of 550 soldiers, 100 sailors, 16 horsemen, 10 brass guns, and 4 small cannons—a tiny band to contest unknown enemies.

The first of Cortés's vessels to arrive at the Yucatán Peninsula was commanded by a hot-tempered officer named Pedro de Alvarado. His ship dropped anchor in front of a silvery white beach near what is today Mexico's vacation playground of Cancún. Cortés had issued orders that no one was to step ashore until all eleven ships had arrived. But Alvarado took a landing party to the beach, captured three local Indians, and looted a fishing village. The Spaniards found only a few specks of gold, and Alvarado decided to torture his three captives to learn where more gold was stored. Then, suddenly, his commander appeared.

On that Yucatán beach, the Spanish soldiers discovered they had a unique captain. Cortés was furious at Alvarado. He demanded that Alvarado release the three Indians and return all their goods. Never, Cortés told his lieutenant, could the Spaniards win the confidence of the Indians if they stole their property. The Spaniards were puzzled by their leader's behavior. Soldiers at the time were commonly paid in "booty"— the goods they looted from conquered lands. But to Cortés, raiding villages was the action of a pirate. Cortés would allow his men to take booty, but not from simple fisher folk.

One morning while they were still on the Yucatán coast, Cortés's men were astonished to find a nearly naked man walking into their camp. He looked like a European, but his skin was burnt black from the

Mayan ruins at Tulum on the Yucatán Peninsula

tropical sun. Most surprising of all, the man spoke to them in Spanish. He was Jeronimo de Aguilar, one of only two survivors of a Spanish crew that had been shipwrecked there seven years earlier. The other Spanish sailor lived in the interior and had gone completely native. He was advising the coastal people that Spaniards were greedy and treacherous and should be driven into the sea.

Aguilar joined Cortés's army and was a welcome addition. He had lived among the natives of a fishing village and knew the Mayan language that was commonly spoken on the Mexican coast. In the months to come, he would be invaluable as an interpreter. Discovering Aguilar was Cortés's first stroke of luck in Mexico. He would be blessed with many more gifts of fortune during his stay.

Statue of Gonzalo Guerrero, the first European to live in Mexico, in Quintana Roo, Mexico

Sunset over the Mayan ruins of Chichén Itzá

Leaving the Yucatán, Cortés sailed south and west along the Mexican shore. At the mouth of the Grijalva River he encountered the Tabascan Indians. These were warriors, not frightened fishermen. On a plain near the river, Cortés fought his first battle in Mexico.

From the beginning, the odds looked hopeless—a few ranks of Spanish infantrymen facing thousands of swarming Tabasco warriors. With drums beating and conch shells blaring, the Tabascans charged. The Spanish musketmen raised their weapons. They fired and several Indian attackers fell in their tracks. Next, a cannon shot ripped down dozens of the warriors. Never before had the Tabascans seen such wonder weapons. Did these white invaders have the power of thunder on their side? Still, the courageous Tabascans pressed forward. They froze in terror, however, when a godlike creature emerged from the trees behind the foot soldiers. Its form was human on the top with a torso, two arms, and a head. But it pranced about on four powerful legs, allowing it to run as fast as the wind.

The Tabascans were seeing a horse for the first time in their lives. To them it was a miracle creature. They believed the horse and the rider were one and the same being. From sheer fright, their attack ground to a halt.

After the battle, Cortés gathered the terrified Tabascans together and attempted to make peace. Using Aguilar as a translator, he asked where he could find gold. He was told that vast amounts of gold lay in a city far to the west across the distant mountains. While pointing inland, the Tabascans blurted out the name of this great city: "Mexico! Mexico!" The Tabascans were referring to Tenochtitlán, called

Xaltelolco.

Mexico by many coastal people. Upon hearing the word, dreams of wealth danced in the Spaniards' minds—Mexico, Mexico, city of gold.

As was their custom, the Tabascans presented the Spaniards with women as gifts. One of the women was only a teenager, but she carried herself with the dignity of a princess. The Spaniards learned she was the daughter of a nobleman who had been sold into slavery to settle a debt. She came to be called Malinche. Eventually Malinche came to live with Cortés. She also rose to become a towering but controversial figure in Mexican history.

Cortés meeting Aztec emissaries with his interpreter, Malinche, by his side

Chapter 3
The World of the Aztecs

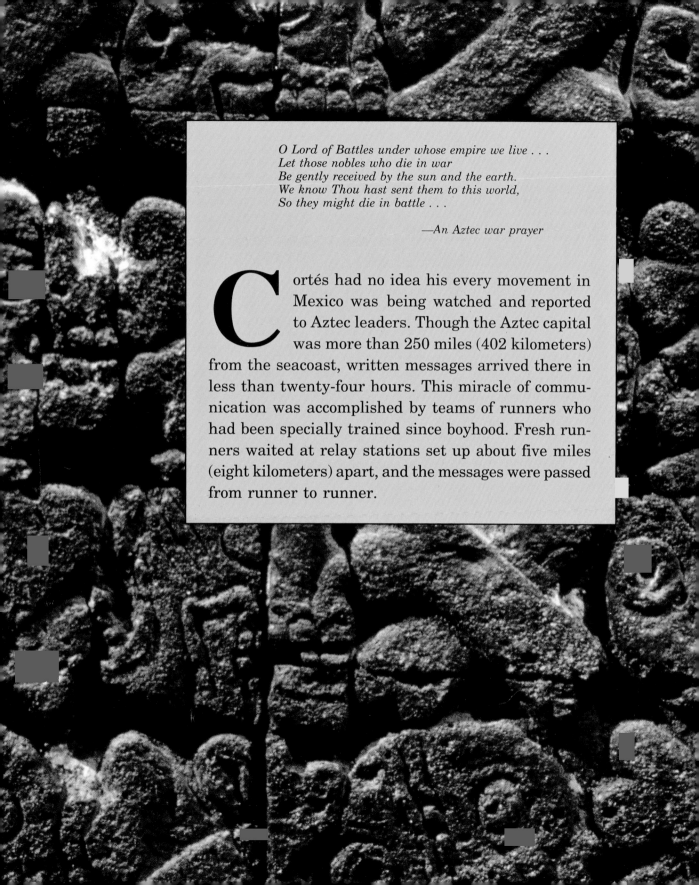

O Lord of Battles under whose empire we live . . .
Let those nobles who die in war
Be gently received by the sun and the earth.
We know Thou hast sent them to this world,
So they might die in battle . . .

—An Aztec war prayer

C ortés had no idea his every movement in Mexico was being watched and reported to Aztec leaders. Though the Aztec capital was more than 250 miles (402 kilometers) from the seacoast, written messages arrived there in less than twenty-four hours. This miracle of communication was accomplished by teams of runners who had been specially trained since boyhood. Fresh runners waited at relay stations set up about five miles (eight kilometers) apart, and the messages were passed from runner to runner.

Mexico's national symbol, an eagle perched on a cactus and devouring a snake, in a stained-glass window of Mexico's Chapultepec Palace

Receiving the messages was the Aztec emperor Moctezuma (sometimes spelled Motecuhzoma or Montezuma). He presided over a kingdom that stretched from the Atlantic to the Pacific and from the deserts of northern Mexico to the jungles of the south. More than fifteen million subjects lived under Aztec control. Moctezuma knew of no other nation that rivaled his in wealth or military might. But Aztec history was rife with legends that an avenging god would someday return to claim all of Mexico as his own. Those legends were older even than the Aztec nation itself.

Traditional Aztec history held that their people originated above the northern deserts in a place called Aztlan. Folktales later portrayed Aztlan as a Garden of Eden. For unknown reasons, the people left Aztlan and began wandering south seeking a new home. Their march lasted more than a century. During the trek they were guided by their chief god Huitzilopochtli, the hummingbird deity. Wherever they trekked, they carried a statue of this hummingbird god in a cagelike enclosure. It was believed that the idol gave directions while whispering into the ear of the tribal priests. The hummingbird god instructed the priests to find a place where they would see an eagle perched on a cactus while eating a snake. On that spot they were to build their capital city.

At last the Aztecs entered the green and fertile Valley of Mexico, where many advanced civilizations thrived. In the valley they marveled at the sprawling stone cities and neat, productive farms. The Aztecs settled in a semi-barren area on the shores of a broad but shallow lake called Texcoco. Having little to offer their sophisticated neighbors, the Aztecs became mercenaries—paid soldiers willing to fight other people's battles. Their experience as mercenaries allowed them to build a ruthlessly efficient army.

Year after year, the Aztecs probed the Valley of Mexico searching for a permanent home. Their historians claim that in the year 1325 they beheld the fulfillment of prophecy. On an island in the middle of Lake Texcoco, they saw an eagle sitting on a cactus while it devoured a snake. Here, indeed, was the promised land. The Aztecs built their capital city on the island. They called the city Tenochtitlán, Place of the Cactus.

As they gained power and overwhelmed their neighbors, the Aztecs acquired skills in engineering, agriculture, and government. In less than one century, they progressed from rootless mercenaries to the mightiest people in Mexico. Their capital city became Mexico's shining jewel. Great pyramids rose in the city's center. Canals carried canoe traffic in orderly, grid-like patterns, like the streets of a modern city. Three broad, concrete causeways connected the island metropolis to the shores of Lake Texcoco. Marveling at the glorious capital, an Aztec poet wrote:

> The city is spread out in circles of jade,
> Radiating flashes of light . . .
> Beside it the lords are borne in boats;
> Over them extends a flowing mist.

Pleasing the gods was the prime activity of the Aztec nation. In the center of the capital rose more than forty pyramids with temples on their peaks. The Aztecs worshiped a rain god, a fire god, a harvest god, and many more. At the top of their pantheon stood Huitzilopochtli, the hummingbird deity. To win the hummingbird's favor and to avoid his wrath, the Aztecs offered human hearts.

Aztec statue of Centeocihuatl, goddess of rich harvests

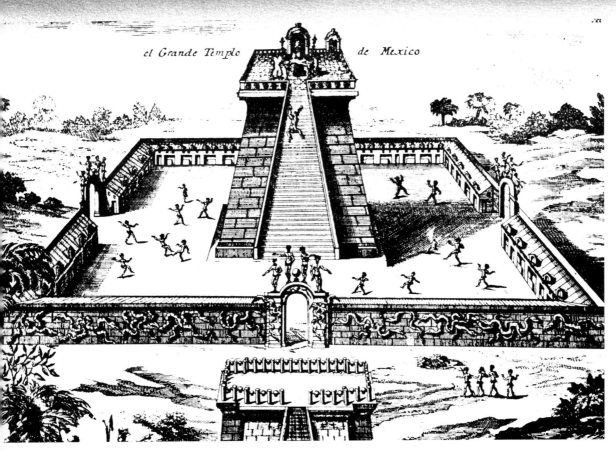

el Grande Templo de Mexico

The Aztec temple at Tenochtitlán

Aztec vase used for holding the sacrificial ashes

Human sacrifice—the ritual killing of men and women in order to please a god—was practiced by many ancient peoples. In Mexico, both highly sophisticated tribes and primitive societies performed sacrificial rites. But no culture took human sacrifice to such extremes as did the Aztecs during the height of their power. When the hummingbird god's pyramid was dedicated in the year 1490, some twenty thousand victims died in front of his temple.

Women and even children were sometimes sacrificed, but most victims were prisoners of war. To supply hearts for their altars, the Aztecs fought "flower wars" with their neighbors. The purpose of a flower war was to capture victims, not to gain territory. The soldier who took an enemy prisoner won far more praise than one who killed his opponent. When no wars were

Carvings at the Aztec temple of Huitzilopochtli

being waged, the Aztecs sent "tax collectors" to vassal tribes to bring back sacrificial victims.

According to Aztec beliefs, the very order of the universe compelled them to practice the bloody sacrificial rites. To the Aztecs, the forces of good and evil were locked in constant war. The morning did not simply follow the night; instead, the sun god battled the darkness. Without human hearts, the god of light might weaken and fail in his struggle, plunging the world into eternal night.

Hungriest of all the gods was Huitzilopochtli, the hummingbird. He had originated as the god of the hunt, but evolved to become the nation's war deity. If the hummingbird became displeased with his people, he would surely sap the strength of Aztec soldiers and cause the collapse of the empire.

Calendar devised by the Aztecs, who were expert astronomers

In the Aztec pantheon reigned one maverick god. He was Quetzalcóatl, the feathered serpent. Legends told of ancient times when the serpent deity lived among various Mexican tribes. He taught the people farming, medicine, and other useful skills. Above all, the serpent deity condemned the practice of human sacrifice. He preferred gifts of beautiful butterflies to bloody human hearts.

Rival gods, it was said, disliked the gentle Quetzalcóatl and drove him from Mexico. According to legends, he was last seen sailing over the eastern ocean on a ship made of snakes. But the feathered serpent vowed he would someday return to claim all of Mexico as his own. Aztec astronomers calculated that Quetzalcóatl would come back in the year One Reed in the Aztec calendar.

Mystery and magic ruled the thinking of Moctezuma, the Aztec emperor. He believed that strange events foretold disaster. In recent months, his nation had been besieged with puzzling incidents. A temple atop the capital's highest pyramid caught fire and burned to ashes. A fiery comet hung in the night sky for weeks. Residents claimed that every night they heard the eerie voice of a weeping woman calling, "Come with me, my children. Come with me."

Then came the ominous reports from the eastern seacoast. Strangers were seen riding in gigantic canoes that looked like mountains on the water. They carried death-dealing weapons and possessed what seemed to be creatures out of a nightmare. And they touched upon Mexican shores in the year One Reed— the same year Quetzalcóatl, the feathered serpent, promised to reclaim the land.

The Aztec god Quetzalcóatl

Chapter 4
The March Inland

"There was among us not one who was not very much afraid, seeing how deep into this country we were and among so many hostile people and so entirely without hope of help from anyone."

—Hernando Cortés, in a letter to King Charles of Spain

On an island near the Mexican coast, Cortés and his men encountered Aztecs for the first time. Moctezuma, whose agents had been anxiously observing the Spaniards since they landed, sent a team of emissaries to talk to their leader. The emissaries came bearing gifts—food, rare feathers, and, to the Spaniards' great delight, objects made from pure gold.

During this first meeting between Cortés and the Aztecs, the importance of the slave girl Malinche became apparent. Malinche spoke Nahuatl, the language of the Aztecs. She also spoke Mayan, which the shipwrecked sailor Aguilar had learned during his years living in a coastal fishing village. Through a complicated exchange of languages, Malinche was able to translate the Aztec words into Mayan, which Aguilar, in turn, put into Spanish.

With the help of Malinche and Aguilar, Cortés told the Aztec emissaries that he wished to go to the capital city and speak with their leader. To impress the Aztecs, Cortés had his horsemen prance about on their miraculous beasts, and he ordered a cannon to fire into a sand dune. He also displayed several Spanish fighting dogs—a breed far larger than any dog found in Mexico. The demonstrations left the Aztec officers trembling in fear.

Before the Aztec emissaries returned to their capital, Cortés gave them a battered old helmet. He suggested they present the helmet to Moctezuma and bring it back filled with gold. Cortés explained, "We Spaniards suffer from a disease of the heart which can only be cured by gold."

Several weeks later the Aztecs reappeared. As Cortés requested, the helmet was now filled with gold nuggets and gold flakes. And the Aztecs brought far more—gold figurines of animals, birds, and fishes, and two huge, exquisitely decorated disks the size of cartwheels; one disk was made of silver, and the other of pure gold. This was by far the richest haul yet taken in the New World.

The Aztec agent told Cortés that the gifts were from Moctezuma himself. He added that the Aztec leader welcomed the Spaniards to Mexico, but under no circumstances were they to come to Tenochtitlán. Cortés studied every piece of the treasure. It only whetted his appetite for more. He told the Aztec officers he represented the king of Spain, a powerful ruler from across the sea. The king insisted that his representative have a face-to-face talk with their chief. Cortés announced he would go to Tenochtitlán, whether he was invited or not.

In April 1519, Cortés's tiny fleet of ships dropped anchor at a fine natural harbor on the Mexican coast. Here Cortés founded the first Spanish town in Mexico. He called it Veracruz (True Cross). Although Cortés claimed the town site and the surrounding land for the king of Spain, he was actually using Spanish law to his advantage. He knew he had a powerful enemy in Diego Velázquez, the governor of Cuba. By founding a Spanish town on his own, Cortés cleverly cut his ties with Velázquez. As mayor of the new town, he declared he was now an agent working directly for the king. Dutifully he dispatched a ship containing one-fifth of the Aztec treasure—the traditional "king's fifth"—and a letter of explanation to King Charles.

Charles, king of Spain

On the Mexican coast, Cortés also met Indians of the Totonac group. Their capital city, Cempoala, lay a short hike from Veracruz. Cempoala was a substantial city of twenty-five thousand people. Its white plastered buildings made the Spaniards dream of silver. The Totonacs greeted the foreigners as friends. Their leader was an enormous man whom the Spaniards nicknamed the "fat cacique." The word cacique originated on the Caribbean islands, and the Spaniards used it when referring to any Indian leader. The fat cacique complained that his people were virtual slaves of the powerful Aztecs. Quickly Cortés grasped

"Totonac Civilization," a mural by Mexican artist Diego Rivera in Mexico City's National Palace

that Moctezuma's vast empire consisted of many vassal states who hated Aztec rule.

As Cortés spoke to the fat cacique, a group of Aztec "tax collectors" happened into the city. Acting as if the Spaniards were not even present, the tax collectors demanded twenty Totonac men to come with them and be sacrificed on the altars of Tenochtitlán. Cortés ordered his soldiers to seize the Aztecs and hold them in chains. By doing this he won the loyalty of the Totonacs. But Cortés was also a clever diplomat. Later he secretly released the Aztec tax collectors. He told them their freedom was an act of friendship granted by the Spanish king. He also asked that they report this charitable act to Moctezuma.

Each morning Cortés spent in the Totonac capital, he witnessed a gruesome ceremony. To the accompaniment of drumbeats, three or four slaves were led to the city's pyramid. There they were stretched out on a sacrificial stone and their hearts were cut out by a high priest. This form of religious murder sickened Cortés and filled his men with dread. Finally Cortés could take no more. He ordered his soldiers to climb the pyramid and topple the bloody sacrificial stone, the altar, and the statues of the gods.

The Totonac people, fearing the wrath of their gods, charged the Spaniards with spears drawn. Cortés grabbed the fat cacique and threatened to kill him if one spear was thrown. Reluctantly the Totonacs dropped their weapons. Cortés then directed his men to build wooden crosses and place them on the vacant pyramid top. When the crosses were in place, he had one of the Spanish priests assigned to his army hold a Mass. The baffled Totonacs looked on, puzzled by this new religion.

Moctezuma, king of the Aztecs

All these activities were observed by Aztec agents and reported to a troubled Moctezuma. What manner of men were the foreigners, he wondered. The leader condemned human sacrifice. Quetzalcóatl, the feathered serpent god of olden times, also opposed human sacrifice. Centuries ago, the feathered serpent god disappeared over the sea to the east. These men came to Mexico from the eastern ocean. Moctezuma worried about another startling parallel between the god and the foreigners. Ancient wall paintings pictured the feathered serpent as a white-faced man with a black beard. The foreign commander was a bearded white man. It all confirmed the awful truth. The Spanish chief was no mere human—he was a god.

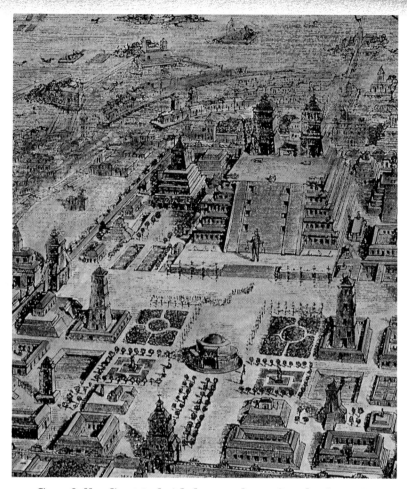

An artist's vision of the Aztec capital of Tenochtitlán

Carefully Cortés laid down plans for the long journey to the Aztec capital city that the coastal people called Mexico. First Cortés moved to erase all thoughts of retreat among his men. As usual, he moved boldly. Before the bulk of his men knew what was happening, Cortés and a tiny band of followers set fire to all his ships. Now, without vessels to carry them back to Cuba, the Spanish soldiers had no choice but to follow their commander. Destroying the ships also freed sailors for service on land.

Leaving a garrison of one hundred men in Veracruz, Cortés led his army west. Included in Cortés's ranks were more than a thousand Totonac warriors, Spain's first allies in Mexico.

By marching toward the Aztec capital, Cortés launched one of the most daring exploration and military missions in history. Ahead lay a country never before seen by European eyes. Cortés would certainly face armies many times larger than his own. But the unknown lands also promised glory and riches. From the time he first arrived in the West Indies as a boy in his teens, Cortés had dreamed of leading a mission such as this. Now, truly, he would meet his destiny. Cortés began this incredible journey in the middle of August, 1519.

Near the coast the Spaniards cut through dense tropical jungle alive with the calling of birds and heavy with the fragrance of flowers. Soon the long column of men pushed uphill through a thick pine forest. At the top of a lofty crest they beheld the mighty Orizaba Mountain, whose peak was snow-covered in both summer and winter. Cortés's Totonac guides had made the journey westward many times and were able to show him the best routes.

Eight days into the trek, the army reached Xocotla, a large city of gleaming, white buildings. By this time the entire countryside buzzed with the news that the foreigners were on the march, and the people stared at the Spaniards and their horses more out of curiosity than surprise. At the city's temple complex, Cortés's men shuddered when they saw a gruesome pile of human skulls. These skulls, all victims of past sacrifice, numbered in the thousands.

In a letter written to the king, Cortés described Mexico's bloody sacrificial rites as "the most terrible and frightful thing we [Spanish soldiers] have ever seen." But, judging from the Spaniards' backgrounds, their disgust with Mexico's bloody religious practices

A family accused of heresy being condemned to death during the Spanish Inquisition

seems puzzling. Cortés and his soldiers lived through the darkest years of the Spanish Inquisition. During the Inquisition, religious fanaticism gripped Spain. People suspected of false religious beliefs were tortured and put to death in slow, agonizing ways. Probably every Spaniard on the march had seen men and women burned at the stake, condemned to that ghastly death by religious authorities who claimed to be acting in the name of God. It could be argued that burning at the stake was a Spanish form of human sacrifice; however, the *conquistadores* failed to see the similarity. To them, sacrifice on pagan altars was proof that the Indians of Mexico were barbarians who deserved to be conquered and enslaved.

41

Cortés next arrived at the mountain nation of Tlaxcala. The Totonacs claimed the Tlaxcalans had been fighting the Aztecs for more than a century, and Cortés thought he would find allies there. Instead, Cortés found himself battling for his life. The Tlaxcalans cleverly allowed the Spaniards to enter their territory before unleashing the fury of a surprise attack. Several Spanish accounts suggest that Cortés's entire army would have been slain on the plains of Tlaxcala had it not been for the enemy's peculiar way of fighting. Tlaxcalan soldiers were accustomed to engaging in "flower wars" with the Aztecs. The object of a flower war was to capture an opponent rather than kill him. Consequently, the Tlaxcalan swordsmen were reluctant to render a fatal blow when they closed in on the Spanish ranks.

Tlaxcalans presenting to Cortés a gift of several beautiful maidens

When the frenzy of battle finally ebbed, a group of Tlaxcalan officers approached Cortés. They said that further fighting would be foolish, and asked if they could be friends. Cortés agreed and the Tlaxcalans later became his most devoted allies.

As Cortés scored victory after victory, a shaken Moctezuma held meetings with this astrologers, high priests, and fortune-tellers. One priest had dreamed the foreigners would never get beyond the city of Cholula. To Moctezuma, this was a prophecy. Cholula was a religious center dedicated to Quetzalcóatl, the feathered serpent. If Cortés was Quetzalcóatl, it would be only fitting for him to meet his death—if indeed he could be killed—in that city. Moctezuma sent out a new emissary, welcoming the Spaniards to Tenochtitlán but insisting they pass through Cholula.

Monastery near Cholula, Mexico

43

After leaving Tlaxcala, Cortés led his army southward through a valley green with corn. Once more he gained allies as six thousand Tlaxcalans joined the Spanish ranks. The Tlaxcalans warned Cortés of Aztec treachery. They claimed the leaders of Cholula were terrified of the Aztecs and would do anything Moctezuma ordered. Cortés, growing more confident as he neared the capital, ignored the warnings.

At the gates of Cholula, the Spaniards were greeted by musicians beating on drums and playing flutes. Children scattered flowers at the visitors' feet. Cortés responded to this courtesy by ordering the Tlaxcalans to camp at the town limits while the Spaniards entered the city. Once settled in Cholula, the Spaniards feasted on turkey, beans, and tortillas.

The hospitality the Spaniards received at Cholula would have lulled them to sleep had it not been for the resourcefulness of the ex-slave girl and interpreter Malinche. During the evening, Malinche joined a gossip session with several Cholula women. One of the women—the wife of a chief—took a liking to her and hoped she would someday marry her youngest son. The woman told Malinche that an army of twenty thousand Aztec warriors was secretly camped outside of town, ready to spring a deadly trap. The battle plan called for Cholula soldiers to strike the Spaniards first and then be joined by the Aztecs. Malinche reported what she had learned to Cortés.

The next morning Cortés calmly asked the Cholula leaders to join him for a discussion. Acting as if he suspected nothing, Cortés requested porters to help carry his equipment. When a huge horde of Cholula men were assembled, Cortés fired a musket shot and triggered a surprise attack of his own.

The battle of Cholula

The result was a massacre. Cannonfire ripped through the lines of closely-packed Cholulans. Arrows and musket shot rained down upon them, fired by Spaniards hidden on rooftops. More than 3,000 Cholula men were killed. The death toll would have been even higher had not Cortés restrained the Tlaxcalans, who killed and looted with reckless delight.

The massacre at Cholula has provoked bitter debate among historians. Many believe there was no Aztec army waiting outside the city, poised to attack. Instead, they argue, the Spaniards were trigger-happy and the Tlaxcalans eager to loot the rich city.

In Tenochtitlán, however, the news from Cholula left Moctezuma stunned. Now more than ever before the Aztec chief was convinced his foe had supernatural powers. What could Moctezuma—a mere mortal—do to stop a god?

Chapter 5
Tenochtitlán

"I stood looking at [Tenochtitlán] and thought, never in the world would there ever again be discovered other such lands as these. . . ."
—*Bernal Díaz del Castillo*

It had been two-and-a-half months since the Spaniards left Veracruz to begin their push inland. They were travel-weary, battle-scarred, and growing more and more frightened as they neared the Aztec capital. Every day the soldiers asked each other how their tiny force—even with the assistance of thousands of Indian allies—could defeat the mighty Aztecs if they had to engage in battle. It was madness, the men claimed, to continue the march. But a determined Hernando Cortés would hear no talk of turning back. Ahead of him lay a new world ripe for conquest.

More than 75 miles (121 kilometers) of rugged mountains separated Cholula from the Valley of Mexico. With Cortés at its head, the slow-moving column wormed westward over the forbidding terrain. Indian guides led the men through a pass between two towering mountains with the tongue-twisting names Popocatepetl and Iztacihuatl. Beyond the pass, a footpath wound down into a valley alive with greenery.

In contrast to the bleak mountains, the Valley of Mexico seemed so lush and beautiful that some Spaniards believed it was enchanted. The army passed through pine forests dotted with shining lakes. In carefully cleared areas spread green fields of corn. Towns popped up around practically every bend in the trail. With a touch of wonder, Bernal Díaz said, "Gazing on such sights, we did not know what to say, or whether what appeared before us was real. . . ."

In the clear mountain air the Spaniards could see for miles. Below sprawled a huge complex of lakes, with the gleaming waters of Lake Texcoco in the center. Three broad causeways led to an island city in the middle of the lake. Here was the Aztec capital that Bernal Díaz called "the great city of Mexico."

Finally the Spaniards stood in front of the northern causeway leading to the island metropolis. Lake Texcoco was filled with hundreds of bobbing canoes as curious Aztecs gazed upon the visitors. Bernardino de Sahagun, a Spanish priest, later interviewed an Aztec who had witnessed Cortés's arrival. According to the Aztec, "Four stags [horses] came first. At the front there was only the banner. The bearer carried it on his shoulders. He shook it and made it move in circles. Following him were those with unsheathed iron swords, the swords shining and glittering."

The causeway was wide enough for eight men to march side by side. As they advanced, the Spaniards were greeted by hundreds of Aztec noblemen dressed in flowing robes and wearing headdresses of rare feathers. The noblemen bent down, touched the ground, and then kissed their hands. This was the traditional Aztec way of welcoming foreign dignitaries. The nobles had been sent to the causeway by Moctezuma. The king had tried everything in his power to prevent the Spaniards from entering his city. Now he was prepared to pay homage to their leader.

Riding at the head of the column, Cortés saw the welcoming committee part. Behind them approached a man carried in a jewel-bedecked litter. Nobles dusted the ground and spread out cotton cloth for him to walk upon. Cortés halted the march and swung off his horse. This man, he knew, was the Aztec king.

Cortés received by Moctezuma

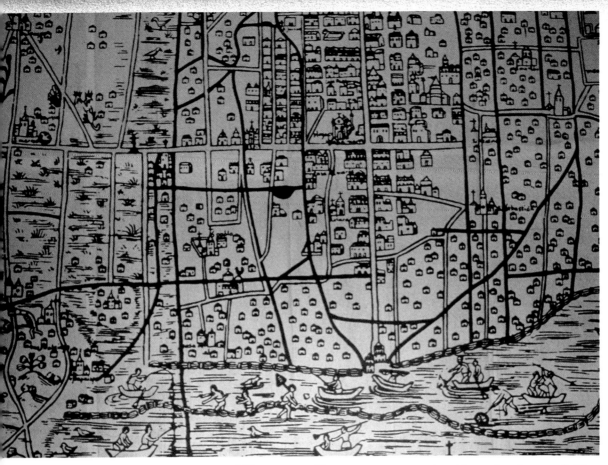

Map of Tenochtitlán

There on the causeway, in the shadow of Tenochtitlán, the leaders of two great cultures—evolved on opposite sides of the world—met for the first time. It was a rare and dramatic moment in history, brought about largely through Cortés's iron will as a soldier and his hunger to discover new lands.

Accounts differ as to the details of this unique meeting. Certainly the two men exchanged gifts. They spoke, with Malinche acting as interpreter. By this time she had mastered many Spanish words. It is not known for certain what the two leaders said, but in a letter to the Spanish king Cortés detailed a conversation he had with Moctezuma later that day. Moctezuma's tone indicates that, upon first meeting Cortés, he believed the Spaniard was a god or at least the

Cortés meeting with Moctezuma at Tenochtitlán

agent of a god: "We have always held that those who descended from [the feathered serpent god] would come and conquer this land and take us as their vassals. So because of the place from which you come, namely from the east where the sun rises, and the things you tell us of the king who sent you here . . . we shall obey you and hold you as our lord."

Inside the city, the Spaniards were housed in a magnificent palace that once belonged to Axayactl, Moctezuma's father. Servants brought them an extravagant meal. So gracious were the Aztecs that they even provided beds of flowers for the Spaniards' horses to sleep on. Still, Cortés took no chances. He posted guards armed with muskets on the palace roof and placed a cannon at the entrance.

Just days after their guests arrived, Aztec leaders took the Spaniards on a tour of the capital city. The first stop was the broad central market. Never before had the Spaniards seen such a wondrous place. In the market, some sixty thousand people bought and sold a fantastic variety of goods. Food vendors offered tortillas, corn cakes, fruit, ducks, fish, and meat from wild pigs or deer. Shoppers browsed through stacks of colorful clothes made from cotton or animal skins. People ate in tiny restaurant stalls. Barbers cut hair. Buyers and sellers exchanged cacao beans, which were used as money as well as to make chocolate.

The Spaniards' attention was drawn to the many gold and silver items sold in the marketplace. The Aztecs used gold for fashioning fine figurines and jewelry, but they valued rare, colorful feathers far more highly. Though the Spaniards were obsessed with gold merely as a source of wealth, they still admired the workmanship of Aztec jewelers and artists. The visitors concluded that Aztec goldsmiths were the equal of any in Europe. In fact, the marketplace itself was vastly superior to counterparts in the Old World. Bernal Díaz noted, "Some of the soldiers among us who had been in many parts of the world, in Constantinople, and all over Italy, and in Rome, said so large a marketplace and so full of people, and so well regulated and arranged, they had never beheld before."

The Aztecs next led their visitors to the temple complex. The Spaniards huffed and panted as they climbed the steps of the city's tallest pyramid. The view from the top was magnificent. All of Lake Texcoco and the fifty or more small towns built on its shores could be seen. The three causeways, which

Aztec woman spinning cotton

Skulls of Aztec sacrificial victims

linked the island city with the shore, radiated outward like the spokes of a wheel. Cortés studied the causeways carefully. Each had removable bridges that were floated away at regular intervals to allow the passage of canoes. Clearly the Aztecs could—if they wished—remove the bridges and strand the Spaniards in the city. Cortés was a man of many minds. And his military mind was always wary of a trap.

The Spaniards, to their horror, also saw the gruesome side of the Aztec temple center. On a rack in a courtyard stood endless rows of human skulls, all staring blankly into eternity. One Spanish soldier, by counting rows and multiplying, claimed he counted 136,000 of them. The skulls were grim reminders that the Aztecs sent more victims to the altars than any other people in Mexico.

The Aztec priests offered the Spaniards, as honored guests, close-up looks at their idols. The Spaniards agreed to the tour, although they were sickened by their surroundings. Around them were statues, sacrificial stones, and walls caked with human blood. Even the priests were frightful sights. Aztec religious law forbade them to bathe or to wash or cut their hair. After years of absorbing sacrificial blood, the priests' hair was matted into tangled red-caked braids. The temple complex reeked from the smell of blood and decaying bodies. Bernal Díaz wrote, "In the slaughterhouses of Spain there is not such another stench."

Aztec tiger altar

Huitzilopochtli, Aztec god of war

Finally the priests took the Spaniards before their principal idol, Huitzilopochtli, the hummingbird deity. This was not the simple stone figure the Aztecs carried through the desert during their nomadic period. This statue was twice the size of a man and had a strangely cold gaze that left some Spaniards trembling. Bernal Díaz claimed "it [Huitzilopochtli] had a very broad face and monstrous and terrible eyes . . . and the body was girded by great snakes."

Next to the hummingbird stood another idol, which Díaz described as having "the face of a bear and glittering eyes made of mirrors."

The Spaniards, shaken by the experience in the temple complex, decided to build a Christian altar in their quarters. While searching the palace for a suitable spot, they discovered a walled-off entrance to what appeared to be a hidden chamber. They broke through the wall and found the fulfillment of their dreams. In the flickering torchlight they saw hundreds of gold ornaments, stacks of gold bars, and baskets full of rare jewels. Bernal Díaz said of the find, "When I saw it I marveled. . . . I took it for certain that there could not be another such store of wealth in the whole world." The Spaniards had stumbled upon the treasure of Axayactl, Moctezuma's father. They had come to the New World and risked their lives in search of treasure such as this.

Cortés ordered his men not to touch the treasure. He also had the secret chamber carefully resealed. There would be time enough in the future to distribute this booty. First he must secure his position in the heart of the Aztec nation.

After his ninth day in the capital, Cortés and a group of his officers made what appeared to be a routine call on Moctezuma. But this visit proved to be far from routine. Angrily Cortés told the Aztec chief he had received word from Veracruz of a battle between Aztecs and Spaniards. During the fighting several Spaniards were killed. Such a skirmish had indeed taken place, but there was no evidence suggesting Moctezuma had instigated it. Then Cortés shocked the Aztec court by declaring Moctezuma to be a prisoner of the Spaniards.

To the surprise of his advisers, Moctezuma received the news of his arrest by weeping. Almost slavishly he agreed to go to the Spanish quarters and to be held prisoner there. His crying soon became uncontrollable.

Moctezuma was at the time forty years old, just a few years older than Cortés. Before becoming emperor, he had been a high-ranking general famed for his bravery on the battlefield. Historians still argue over why he allowed himself so timidly to be taken captive. Surely by this time he knew the Spaniards were not gods nor even emissaries of the gods. They ate, they slept, they bled and walked the earth just like other men.

Perhaps Moctezuma's resolve was weakened by some fatalistic vision that told him that, even if these Spaniards went away, more would surely follow. Or perhaps Moctezuma was simply overwhelmed by Cortés's boldness. This man—though outnumbered almost one thousand to one—simply marched up to the Aztec chief and arrested him.

For the next six months Cortés ruled the Aztec empire. Moctezuma, a cooperative prisoner, told the people to obey the commands of their new Spanish overlord. Minor chiefs were given day-to-day instructions through Cortés's interpreter, Malinche, who had suddenly become the most powerful woman in Aztec history.

Although Moctezuma remained under arrest, he was free to roam the Spanish quarters. A strange friendship developed between prisoner and jailer. Cortés spoke of the imprisoned leader as "my true brother." Moctezuma taught the Spaniard how to play an Aztec dice game called totoloque, and the two whiled away the hours in good-natured gambling. When a Spanish soldier insulted the Aztec chief, Cortés had the man flogged.

Spaniards destroying Mexican idols

During his six-month reign, Cortés attempted to impose Christianity on the Aztec people. Cortés was a devout Catholic who went to Mass every morning. He ordered his men to climb to the pyramid tops and topple the Aztecs' idols. He also forbade human sacrifice in the capital. Writing to the Spanish king, Cortés said, "The principal idols . . . I overturned from their seats and rolled down the stairs . . . which grieved Moctezuma and the natives not a little."

The army's priest, Bartolome de Olmedo, found the Aztecs to be willing listeners to the message of Christ. However, he failed to convince the Aztec people that Christianity was the only true and universal religion. The priest soon realized that the people were

Spaniards executing Indians, from a drawing by the explorer Samuel de Champlain in his book Voyage to the West Indies and Mexico

willing to honor Christ and the saints, but only as additions to their old pantheon. The Aztecs had a long tradition of borrowing gods from their neighbors. Adopting the new Christian deity fitted in readily with their religious practices.

Cortés was a cruel monarch when he determined harsh measures were necessary. At the start of his reign, he ordered seventeen Aztec soldiers who were involved in the Veracruz fighting to be burned alive in the public square. Thousands of city people gathered to witness the brutal punishment. The Aztec spectators, though long accustomed to bloodletting in their temples, were reduced to stunned silence at the sight of bound men being tossed like logs onto a raging fire.

Still, early in Cortés's regime, there were no attempts to overthrow Spanish rule. For generations the Aztec people had been molded into a highly disciplined military society. In their nation, orders were followed with mindless obedience, and rebellion was an unthinkable act.

By April 1520, Cortés had been in Mexico for less than a year and a half. In that brief period he had fought large-scale and minor battles, always emerging victoriously. He had taken the Aztec capital and subdued that vast empire without firing a shot. His unbroken series of triumphs was astonishing. But he would soon suffer a reversal that came from the hands of his own people.

In Cuba, Governor Diego Velázquez suspected his one-time lieutenant was carving out his own empire and refusing to share the gold or the glory. To punish the upstart Cortés, Velázquez assembled the largest Spanish army ever seen in the New World. The force consisted of more than 1,400 men and many horses. Commanding the soldiers was Pánfilo de Narváez, whose orders were to capture Cortés and bring him back in chains.

The news that Narváez's ships had anchored off Veracruz came to Cortés at a perilous time. Over the past few weeks, Aztec chiefs had been grumbling that Moctezuma had lost his mind and that it was their duty to drive the Spaniards out of Mexico. Leader of the rebel chiefs was Cuauhtémoc, Moctezuma's nephew. He told fellow chiefs that the Aztec gods demanded they remove the Spaniards and re-establish their old religion.

Cortés feared the Spanish army on the coast more than he did a possible Aztec uprising. Leaving his lieutenant, Pedro de Alvarado, in charge of the capital, Cortés took two hundred men and marched toward Veracruz. The decision to place Alvarado in command was the first disastrous mistake Cortés made while in Mexico.

Pedro de Alvarado was perhaps the finest fighting officer in Cortés's army, but he often made snap decisions that led to calamity. It was he who disobeyed Cortés at the start of the expedition and went ashore on the Yucatán Peninsula before all the fleet had arrived at the coast.

Cortés marching off to battle the army of Narváez

One night shortly after Cortés left for Veracruz, Alvarado and his men watched an Aztec celebration. The Spaniards were uneasy. All had heard talk of an Aztec rebellion, and their numbers were cut in half due to Cortés's mission to the coast. The Aztec fiesta that night was a special one to honor Huitzilopochtli, who, among his many roles, was the nation's war god. In the public courtyard, warriors danced while a man beat the giant snakeskin drum that stood atop the highest pyramid. That same drum was used to accompany human sacrifice. Bernal Díaz claimed it made "the most accursed sound and the most dismal that it was possible to invent."

Aztec priests on the top of their temple sounding the snakeskin drum dedicated to the god of war

The Aztec sacrificial stone

A wave of panic swept the Spaniards as they watched the celebration. Man to man, they whispered that the dancing was a prelude to revolution. The Aztec soldiers were preparing to rise up, seize the Spaniards, and offer them as victims to the terrible god Huitzilopochtli. No evidence existed that the Aztecs planned an uprising that night, but the rumor alone terrified Alvarado's men. As the massive drum pounded, they imagined themselves being held on the sacrificial stone and seeing as their last sight on this earth a bloodstained priest poised with a knife at their chest. Many Spaniards believed that dying on a pagan altar would condemn their souls to an eternity of hell's fires.

Aztec sacrificial knife

While the drum continued to thunder, the hot-blooded Pedro de Alvarado sprang into action. He ordered his men to draw their swords and attack the dancers. An Aztec account reads: "They assaulted the man who was drumming and struck off his arms. . . . They beheaded some [warriors] or split their heads to pieces. . . . There was no escape. The blood of warriors flowed like water gathered into pools."

The people of Tenochtitlán were thunderstruck. The Spaniards had killed young men who were unarmed and who had done them no harm. Picking up spears, clubs, and stones, a furious mob of Aztecs raced to the courtyard. The Spaniards fled back to the palace of Axayactl. There they were able to defend the walls with their firearms, but they could not venture outside. They were prisoners in their own palace.

The Spaniards besieged in their own quarters by the Aztecs

The army of Pánfilo de Narváez surrendering to Cortés

Meanwhile, Cortés enjoyed tremendous success on Mexico's coast. First, he had men who were loyal to him infiltrate Narváez's camp. Then he launched an attack at night and captured Narváez with little bloodshed. When the noise of battle faded, Cortés spoke to the men. He knew the newly arrived Spaniards were soldiers of fortune, just as he was. In glowing terms he told of the gold that awaited them all at the Aztec capital. Among his many talents, Cortés was a superb salesman. At the Mexican coast he persuaded the army sent to destroy him to join him instead.

With the addition of Narváez's men, Cortés quadrupled his Spanish force. He also gained scores of cannon and hundreds of horses. Now Cortés's army seemed to be truly invincible. But he had no inkling of the disaster that had befallen Tenochtitlán.

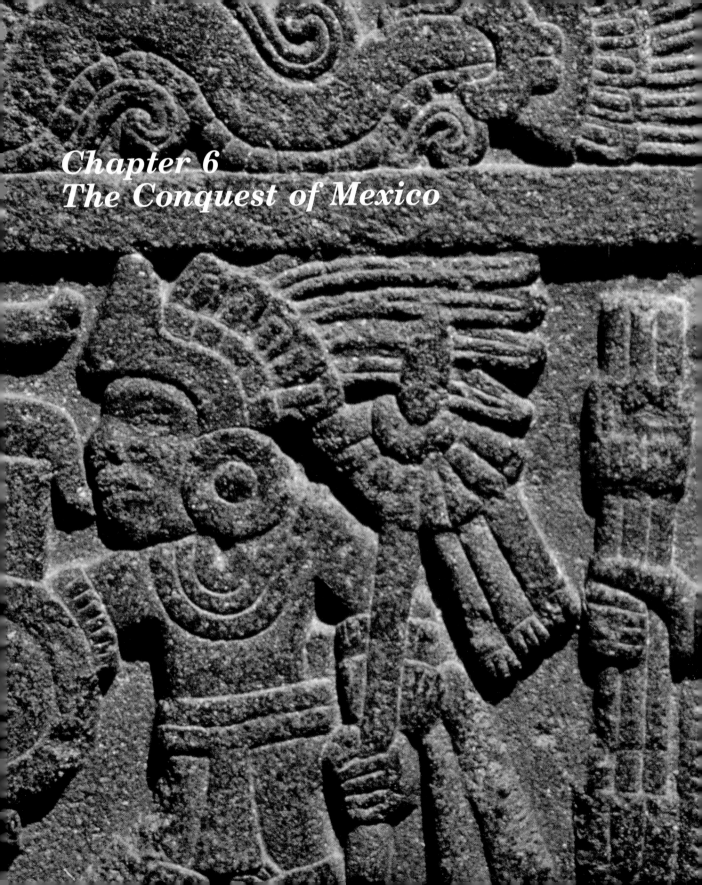

Chapter 6
The Conquest of Mexico

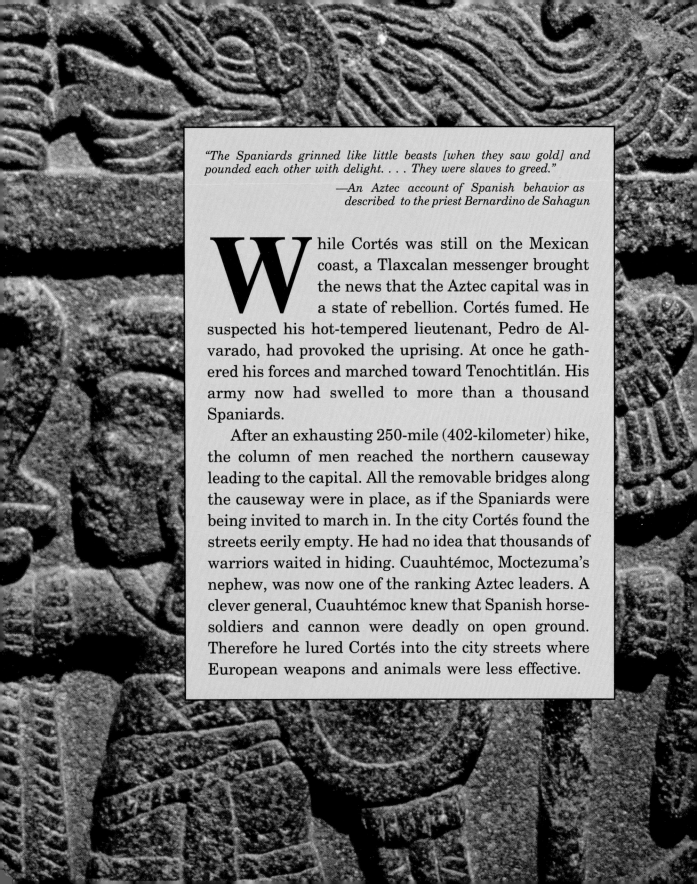

While Cortés was still on the Mexican coast, a Tlaxcalan messenger brought the news that the Aztec capital was in a state of rebellion. Cortés fumed. He suspected his hot-tempered lieutenant, Pedro de Alvarado, had provoked the uprising. At once he gathered his forces and marched toward Tenochtitlán. His army now had swelled to more than a thousand Spaniards.

After an exhausting 250-mile (402-kilometer) hike, the column of men reached the northern causeway leading to the capital. All the removable bridges along the causeway were in place, as if the Spaniards were being invited to march in. In the city Cortés found the streets eerily empty. He had no idea that thousands of warriors waited in hiding. Cuauhtémoc, Moctezuma's nephew, was now one of the ranking Aztec leaders. A clever general, Cuauhtémoc knew that Spanish horse-soldiers and cannon were deadly on open ground. Therefore he lured Cortés into the city streets where European weapons and animals were less effective.

Soon after the Spaniards entered Axayactl's palace where Alvarado was barricaded, the streets outside rang with howling Aztec battle cries. Cortés and his men found themselves surrounded by thousands of warriors. Time after time the Spaniards tried to break out of the palace, but were driven back by furious Aztec assaults. "We killed and wounded many of their soldiers," wrote Bernal Díaz, "yet they managed to reach us by pushing forward over the points of our swords . . . never desisting from their brave attack."

Cortés dragged the captive Moctezuma to the palace roof and ordered him to dismiss the warriors. Moctezuma broke into a fit of sobbing and claimed he only wanted to die. Finally the Aztec chief, who was once revered as a god, tried to speak to the crowd. He was bombarded with a shower of stones. One stone struck him on the head, and—according to the Spanish version of the incident—Moctezuma died three days later. Aztec sources claim that Moctezuma was executed by the Spaniards while still a prisoner.

The situation inside the palace walls grew more perilous each day. The Spaniards had no food and little water. Aztec soldiers shot flaming arrows at the palace and rolled blazing logs to the doors. Said Bernal Díaz, "We were staring death in the face."

Cortés hatched a desperate plan to escape at night. He knew the bridges along the causeway had been removed. So the commander ordered his men to build portable bridges from wooden beams. The gold found in the hidden chamber was brought out, and the soldiers were invited to take what they could carry. Cortés's veterans preferred to travel light, but the recruits from Narváez's army loaded their packs and their pockets with the precious metal.

Moctezuma—by Spanish accounts, wounded by his own people; by native accounts, killed by the Spaniards.

Night fell and a heavy rain drenched the capital. Under the cover of darkness and the storm, the Spaniards made their way through the streets. But upon reaching the causeway, they were detected by a sentry. Soon the evening stillness was shattered by a deafening boom from the snakeskin war drum.

Suddenly the Spaniards were caught in a whirlwind of Aztec warriors. Above them the hellish drum continued to thunder. With nowhere to retreat, the soldiers raced across the causeway. The portable bridge they carried jammed at the first opening. Desperately they rushed to the next gap, plunged into the water, and tried to swim. Greed killed. Those who had overburdened themselves with gold sank like stones.

The battle for the three-mile-long (five-kilometer-long) causeway became a rout. Screaming in terror, the Spaniards ran from one causeway breach to another. Often those who managed to cross the gaps did so on the bodies of their fellow soldiers. As the Spaniards ran, Aztecs in canoes reached out of the darkness, trying to grab their feet and pull them into the water. Never before had even the veteran soldiers suffered through such a nightmare in battle.

An exhausted Hernando Cortés finally reached the shore at the end of the causeway. He had lost almost a thousand Spanish soldiers. Practically all the gold they had taken from the Aztec capital was now on the lake bottom. Cortés sat under a huge cypress tree and wept. It was June 30, 1520. Ever afterward, that evening was called *La Noche Triste*—The Sad Night.

Cortés fighting for his life on the night known as La Noche Triste

While still being harassed by Aztec army units, Cortés gathered his surviving soldiers and began a march to Tlaxcala. As they limped away from the capital region, the Spaniards heard the pounding of the city's enormous snakeskin drum. All knew the terrible meaning of the beats. The men taken prisoner on the mad dash over the causeway the night before were now being sacrificed to the god of war.

The Spanish army was just a shadow of its former self as Cortés led the trek to Tlaxcala. Most of their cannon, crossbows, and muskets had been lost. Practically every member of the army—now numbering about four hundred men—nursed wounds. Fewer than twenty horses remained alive. The men were forced to live on wild cherries they found growing along the roadside.

The tree of La Noche Triste, *a great cypress many centuries old. According to legend, Cortés stopped beneath this tree on the night of his defeat and cried as he saw so many of his men dying.*

As they entered the valley of Otumba, Cortés and his ragtag army saw a chilling sight. Thousands of Aztec warriors waited there to deliver the foreign invaders a final crushing defeat. So many soldiers had been amassed that their ranks disappeared on the horizon. Cortés's men said their prayers, and many wept openly. The Spaniards were so battered they could barely walk, much less fight. Now, facing more enemy soldiers than they had ever seen before, they felt certain they would die on soil far from home.

Cortés shouted to the men to stop their whimpering and to fight like gods. Only his iron will pulled the Spaniards through the exhausting two-hour battle that followed. At one point, Cortés charged his horse into

Cortés at the battle of Otumba

Cortés announcing to his cheering soldiers that he will lead them to victory and fortune

the thick of Aztec ranks, reached the general who was directing the warriors, and killed him with a single swipe of his sword. The Aztecs, without a leader, fell back. López de Gómara, Cortés's biographer, wrote, "the Spaniards who that day saw Hernando Cortés in action swear that never did a man fight as he did . . . and that he alone saved them all."

At Tlaxcala Cortés was greeted as if he were a returning hero. The Tlaxcalans and other tribes so hated the Aztecs that they were willing to fight side-by-side with the Spaniards until victory or death. Cortés made camp at Tlaxcala, and his men tended to their many wounds.

With the exception of recent months, Cortés's adventure in Mexico had been blessed by astonishingly good luck. He had been lucky to find a skillful translator and close friend in Malinche. A series of lucky coincidences had convinced Moctezuma that Cortés was a god. While the Spaniards camped at Tlaxcala, the old Cortés luck returned. The Spanish presence in Mexico was by then almost two years old. Ships had carried word of Mexico's riches to Spanish fortune-hunters throughout the West Indies. As these Spanish freebooters landed at Veracruz, Cortés's officers hurried them to their commander's camp. By December 1520, Cortés's army had increased to nine hundred Spanish troops, one hundred horses, and guns and ammunition.

Buoyed with these new forces, Cortés first acted to protect his lifeline with Veracruz. Tribal leaders along the route were made to swear allegiance to Cortés. If they refused, their cities were sacked and burned. Cortés's Tlaxcalan allies took particular delight in killing or enslaving those people who resisted the Spaniards. With his rear position secured, Cortés next turned his attention to the Aztec capital.

Unknown to Cortés, a calamity had struck Tenochtitlán. Smallpox was now rampant in the island city. Spanish sources say the killer disease was carried to the Aztec capital by one of Narváez's soldiers. Hundreds of years earlier, smallpox epidemics had killed masses of people in the Old World, but Europeans gradually developed a resistance to the sickness. When Spaniards of Cortés's time contracted smallpox, the disease left their faces badly scarred, but it rarely killed them. The people in the New World had no such resistance. Natives of the West Indian islands had

Bronze cannon used by Cortés in Mexico

already been ravaged by the disease. In the decades to come, smallpox and other sicknesses brought over by the whites devastated the Indian population of the American continent.

An Aztec account of the horror in the capital reads: "It [smallpox] began to spread, striking everywhere in the city and killing many people. Sores erupted on their faces, breasts, bellies. They had so many painful sores over their bodies that they could not move, not even turn over in their beds, and if someone tried to move them they screamed in agony. This pestilence killed untold numbers of people, many of them dying because there was no one to feed them, so they starved. Those who survived had holes in their faces, or they were left blinded."

While the epidemic weakened and killed the people inside the city, their outside enemy appeared once more. Cortés arrived at the shores of Lake Texcoco on the day after Christmas, 1520. With his Spanish army was an Indian force numbering twenty thousand men.

First Cortés marched around the rim of the lake, subduing important cities such as Texcoco, Coyoacán, and Tacuba. When the lake region was solidly in Spanish hands, Cortés launched the next stage of his invasion plans, using ships of his own, unique navy.

While the Spaniards were still in Tlaxcala, Cortés commissioned one of his men, an experienced shipwright, to build a dozen war boats called brigantines. Though small by oceangoing standards, these craft

Early map of Mexico City, showing the island city with its bridges, or causeways, to the mainland

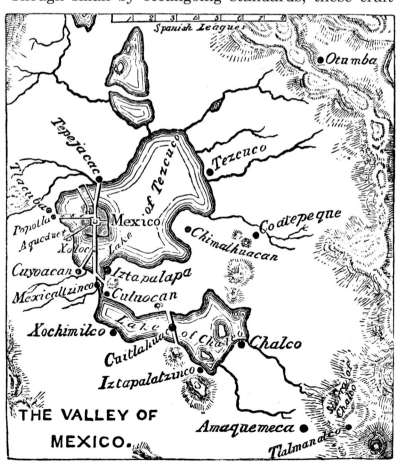

were far larger and more powerful than the Aztec canoes. Cortés well remembered the devastation done by Aztec warriors in canoes during *La Noche Triste*. In the coming battle, he was determined to have command of the lake.

The brigantines were built, then taken apart and carried piece by piece over the mountains. Finally they were reassembled on the shores of Lake Texcoco. On the water, the brigantines could be handled marvelously. They were powered both by oar and by sail and were far faster than any Aztec craft. Gliding smoothly over the lake, the powerful ships were able to ram Aztec canoes and dash them to pieces. The brigantines soon held sway over Lake Texcoco.

Portrait of Cortés

Cortés launched his main land attack on June 9, 1521. At his command, Spanish and Indian soldiers advanced over the southern and western causeways, while another Spanish unit secured the northern causeway to prevent a possible Aztec retreat. One of the epic battles in human history began.

The Aztecs fought with all the tenacious courage that made them masters of Mexico. Day after day the Spaniards battled their way up the causeways, only to be pushed back by ferocious Aztec counterattacks. The grueling combat focused on the causeway breaches. Under protection of Spanish gunners, Tlaxcalan laborers filled in the breaches so the horse-soldiers could advance. But invariably the Aztecs drove the Spaniards backward and opened the breaches once more.

Directing the Aztec resistance was Cuauhtémoc, Moctezuma's nephew. He became a familiar sight, placing his men in the teeth of Spanish advances and encouraging them to fight till death. The Spaniards grudgingly grew to admire their brave foe.

Whenever possible, the Aztecs took prisoners—eighteen Spaniards captured one day, fifty-three taken the next. The prisoners suffered the dreaded fate of being sacrificed to Huitzilopochtli, the war god. These ordeals at the altar were particularly horrifying for the Spaniards still engaged in battle. As they fought at the city's outskirts, they could see their fellow soldiers being ritualistically killed on the pyramid tops. The captives' screams rang out between beats of the terrible sacrificial drum.

Bernal Díaz remembered his comrades suffering the ordeal of human sacrifice and wrote: "I consider myself a good soldier . . . [but] when I saw my companions sacrificed, their hearts taken out still beating

*Cuauhtémoc, nephew of Moctezuma
and last emperor of the Aztecs*

. . . I was truly afraid that one day it might happen to me. They had already seized me twice to take me to be sacrificed, and it pleased God that I escaped. . . . But since then I fear death more than ever."

After weeks of bloody fighting, the Spaniards secured strategic positions on the island city. The Aztecs fought savagely for every inch of ground. During one battle Cortés was pulled off his horse by dozens of warriors and carried toward the pyramid to be sacrificed. At the last moment he was rescued by one of his officers, who rode through the swarms of Aztecs to drag the captain from the enemy's grasp.

Cortés determined that the Aztec capital city had to be razed to the ground, for every house, great and small, provided cover for defenders. The decision to level Tenochtitlán weighed heavy on his conscience. He had dreamed of preserving this great city to be the headquarters of a new Spanish empire. Now it deeply saddened him to destroy the wonderful place he had discovered.

The final stages of the battle were the most brutal time for Tenochtitlán's citizens. The city was completely surrounded, and the people were cut off from food and fresh water. According to an Aztec report: "The people were tormented by hunger, and many starved to death. There was no fresh water to drink, only stagnant water of the lake. . . . The only food was lizards, swallows, corncobs, and salt grasses. . . . Nothing can compare with the horrors of that siege and the agonies of the starving. We were so weakened by hunger that, little by little, the enemy forced us to retreat. Little by little, they forced us to the wall."

The battle for Tenochtitlán lasted for two-and-a-half months. Finally, on August 13, 1521, a brigantine captured a canoe with the Aztec leader Cuauhtémoc aboard. Without a chief, the Aztec resistance collapsed. Cuauhtémoc was taken to Cortés. The Aztec leader asked the Spaniard to take a dagger and kill him. Cortés promised his foe he would not be harmed. The Spanish commander later wrote, "Thus, with this lord a prisoner, the war ceased. . . ."

The weeks of constant battle left Tenochtitlán a city of the dead. Corpses covered the streets and choked the canals. "We could not walk," said Bernal Díaz, "without treading on the bodies and heads of dead Indians." More than two-thirds of the capital's 200,000

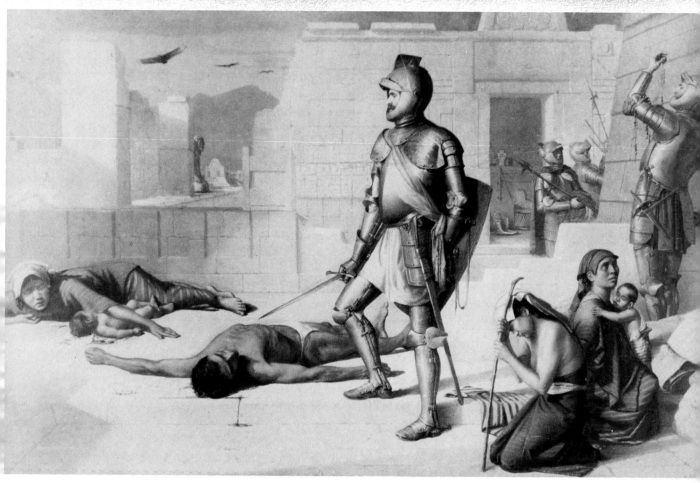

The conquistadors having their way with the Aztecs

inhabitants had died during the siege. The stench of rotting bodies was so terrible that the Spaniards had to retire from the city until Indian laborers disposed of the dead.

Tenochtitlán, which was once too beautiful to be believed, was a shambles. Bernal Díaz claimed, "The city looked as if it had been plowed up." Smoke from a hundred different fires poured out of the marketplace, the temple complex, and the housing areas. A sudden thunderstorm drenched the fires. The rain ceased, revealing a smoldering ash heap. More than Aztec civilization died in those ruins. History was also written in the ashes, as Indian power over Mexico wilted and a new Spanish dominion was born.

Chapter 7
New Spain

"They do nothing but command. . . . They come out very poor from Spain, carrying only a sword. But in a year they have gotten together more goods than a drove of animals can carry, and they insist upon having the houses of gentlemen."
—*Frey Toribio de Benavente, a Spanish priest who complained about immigrants entering Mexico soon after the Aztec conquest*

Cortés's soldiers had risked their lives battling the Aztecs. After victory, the soldiers looked to their leader for rewards. They expected gold. Mexico would prove to be rich in gold and silver; however, the metals lay deep in the hills. Mines had to be dug before the wealth of Mexico was realized. At this point Cortés suspected the country had little treasure that could be taken as booty. But he feared his soldiers would mutiny unless he made some dramatic effort to meet their demands.

Diego Rivera's painting of the tortures of Cuauhtémoc

Cortés called Cuauhtémoc and other surviving Aztec leaders before him. They claimed all the gold the Aztec nation once possessed was in Axayactl's palace and had already been seized by the Spaniards. Those gold items had been lost in Lake Texcoco the night the Spanish soldiers fled the city. Since the fighting ended, divers had tried without success to recover the treasure. The Spanish soldiers were unsatisfied with the Aztecs' answer. Cortés allowed the Aztec leaders to be tortured. Cuauhtémoc's feet were plunged into a bed of red-hot coals. Despite his agony, he revealed nothing about the missing treasure.

Having no gold with which to pay his men, Cortés rewarded them with land and Indian laborers. Thus he brought to Mexico the encomiendo system that was used in the West Indies. Under this system, Spanish soldiers received huge tracts of land called en-

Samuel de Champlain's drawing of Spaniards punishing West Indies natives for not attending church

comiendos. Their ownership contracts included even the Indian people living on the land. Establishing encomiendos made the Spaniards slave-masters over many thousands of Indians. Any Indian who resisted enslavement was tortured or put to death.

Principal to the encomiendo system was the requirement that Spanish landowners give Christian instructions to their Indian workers. For the most part, the requirement was heeded. Although the Spaniards virtually enslaved the Indians, they still considered themselves to be missionaries of Christ. The Indians acceded to their masters' wishes by outwardly accepting Christian beliefs. But in secret, the Indians clung to their old faith. For generations after the conquest, Indian families kept hidden idols in their houses, and when no Spanish overseer was present, they worshiped in their ancient ways.

Cortés's home in Mexico

Cortés had seen the encomiendo system so demoralize the West Indies islanders that the people simply weakened and died. To prevent this from happening in Mexico, he issued a list of regulations. The Tlaxcalans and other tribes that had been allies of the Spaniards would keep their land and their freedom. Indians on the encomiendos could be worked only three weeks out of every seven. But these laws were generally ignored. Many Spaniards worked their Indian laborers to death.

Taking advantage of the encomiendo system, Cortés made huge land claims, mainly south of Mexico City near present-day Cuernavaca. The valley land near Cuernavaca was fertile and well watered, and enjoyed a gentle climate year round. In all, Cortés owned

Detail of Diego Rivera's painting
"The Arrival of Cortés, 1519"

some 25,000 square miles (64,750 square kilometers) of property and had authority over countless Indians. From Spain he brought in cotton, wheat, and cattle, and soon the land yielded rich harvests. He also opened gold mines on his lands. In time Cortés became the richest Spaniard on earth, except for the king.

In his letters to Spain, Cortés asked for priests to come to Mexico, but only those who were "holy men of good life and example." The church dispatched twelve friars of the Franciscan order who were so humble they walked barefoot all the distance from Veracruz to the old Aztec capital. Cortés greeted the friars by dropping to his knees and kissing their robes. The Indian people were overwhelmed by this display of reverence on the part of the great conqueror.

Cortés threw himself into the task of rebuilding the Aztec capital. The Spaniards now called the ruined metropolis Mexico City. A church was built on the site where the great pyramid of Huitzilopochtli once stood. In front of the church spread a broad plaza that soon became lined with shops, houses, and government offices. Hundreds of thousands of Indian laborers toiled to build these structures. Mexico City rose with astonishing speed. One Spanish friar wrote, "More people worked in building the great city than upon the Temple of Jerusalem in Solomon's time."

Ruins of the Cortés family monastery in Cuilapan, Mexico

Cortés's armor

The finest houses in Mexico City belonged to Cortés's followers. Foot soldiers were given half-acre (one-fifth-hectare) plots, while officers built comfortable houses on grounds up to three acres (1.2 hectares) in size. Even men who owned a vast encomiendo in the countryside kept a house in Mexico City. Cortés's house, which stood on the plaza, was ten times larger than any of his neighbors' homes. Often the building stones for Spanish houses came from wrecked pyramids and other Aztec structures. Just three years after the Aztec conquest, Cortés boasted that Mexico City "looks very beautiful [and] will be the most noble and prosperous city [in the known world]."

The conquerors called their empire New Spain, a name first suggested by Cortés. Mexico City served as New Spain's capital. Cortés was the Spanish colony's first governor. Much of New Spain's territory was unexplored or remained under the control of Indians hostile to the whites. But Veracruz and Mexico City became well established, and hundreds of new Spanish immigrants arrived each week. In the countryside Spanish towns sprouted up, with an Old World appearance that they retain even to this day.

From the beginnings, black people played a major role in the building of New Spain. Black workers arrived with the first soldiers commanded by Cortés. During the first twenty years of New Spain's existence, more blacks than whites came to the colony. The majority of blacks arriving in New Spain were slaves of African descent brought from Cuba. Though they were slaves, the blacks often served as field bosses over Indian laborers on the encomiendos.

For Cortés, the conquest of old Tenochtitlán was only the beginning of his New World claims. He had the heart of an explorer and forever hungered to probe into undiscovered lands. Immediately after the conquest, the rebuilding effort compelled him to stay near Mexico City. So instead of leading exploration efforts himself, he sent out parties of discovery. His lieutenant, Pedro de Alvarado, led a mission south into Guatemala. During this expedition, Alvarado founded the city of Oaxaca in southern Mexico. Another officer, Cristobal de Olid, explored Mexico's southwest and reached the Pacific Ocean. Acting under Cortés's orders, Olid built ships and sailed the Pacific coast. Dreaming the dream of Columbus, Cortés hoped to find a seaway for European trade to the Far East.

Cortés instructed the officers he sent on these missions of discovery to treat the native peoples with respect, but his wishes were generally ignored. Although they dutifully claimed land for New Spain, the exploration leaders sought gold for themselves. Ever since they first saw Aztec treasure, Spaniards became spellbound by stories that fabulous wealth lay somewhere nearby. When the Spanish explorers found no gold in the villages they encountered, they believed the people had hidden their treasure. They tortured and killed to learn the location of the secret hoards.

Tropical forest on the Yucatán Peninsula

Cortés served as New Spain's governor for three years. He was the most powerful man in the New World, but he still had as an enemy Diego Velázquez, the governor of Cuba. Velázquez was passionately jealous of the younger man's success in Mexico.

Governor Velázquez had agents in Spain who suggested to King Charles that Cortés was disloyal to the Spanish crown. Other detractors accused Cortés of murdering his Spanish wife, who died mysteriously shortly after her arrival in Mexico City. It was also claimed that Cortés poisoned an agent of the king, who died within days of coming to New Spain's capital. A deadly combination of old enemies and treachery among his own officers led to Cortés's downfall.

In 1524, Cortés sent Cristobal de Olid on an exploration mission south to Honduras. The land there was

1754 map of the lands surrounding the Gulf of Mexico; Mexico is on the left and Cuba in the center

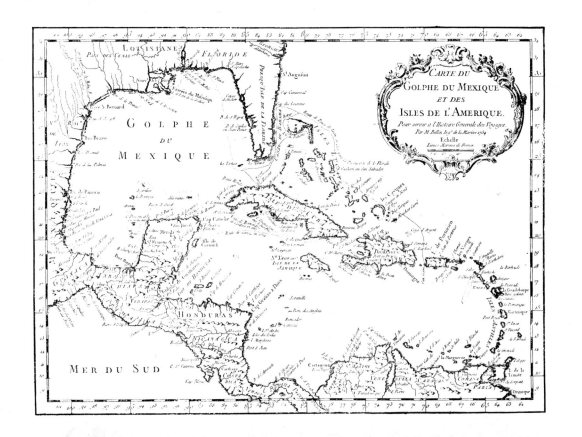

thought to be rich in gold. Olid had participated in the Aztec conquest and believed his efforts were never properly rewarded. Before sailing to Honduras he diverted his ships to Cuba, where he conferred with Governor Velázquez. The two agreed to divide the riches that might be found in Honduras and to deny Cortés a share.

Cortés exploded in rage when he got wind of the plot between Velázquez and Olid. He sent out an army to find Olid and execute him, but months went by and Cortés heard nothing from the army commander. He longed to punish Olid himself, and would tolerate no further waiting. Gathering an army of several hundred Spaniards and thousands of Indians, Cortés began a march to Honduras. He had only scant knowledge of the hideous land that lay before him.

Spanish explorers preparing for an expedition to the Cuban gold mines

The thick Mexican jungle

In the south, jungle growth was so thick that the men were unable to see the ground upon which they walked. When passing through the present-day Mexican state of Tabasco, the army was forced to cross fifty major rivers. The highlands were even more deadly than the jungles. There the men picked their way along tiny footpaths that skirted dizzying cliffs. Most of their horses were lost to falls off the mountain passes.

Food supplies dwindled to practically nothing. Indian soldiers began dropping from starvation. As hunger and hopelessness gripped the army, a frightful rumor passed from Spaniard to Spaniard. The Indian troops were planning to commit mutiny! They intended to kill all the Spaniards!

A shaken Cortés demanded to talk with Cuauhtémoc. He had taken Cuauhtémoc on the mission because he feared leaving him behind would invite rebellion among the Aztecs who lived near Mexico City. Cuauhtémoc, still limping from Cortés's previous torture, claimed there was no truth in the rumors of mutiny. Cortés accused him of lying and ordered him to be hung from a jungle tree. Bernal Díaz, who usually praised his commander, called the execution "a most unjust and cruel sentence."

It took the haggard army almost eighteen months to reach Honduras. There Cortés discovered that Olid had been executed by the first army unit he sent out. The entire Honduras operation was unnecessary. Cortés returned north by ship. When he arrived at Veracruz, he was told that Mexico City was in chaos.

Illustration of Cortés's exploits in Mexico

Because of the Honduran fiasco, Cortés had been absent from Mexico City for almost two years. Officials in the capital believed he was dead. One resident, who claimed to have spiritual powers, said he saw a vision of Cortés's ghost burning in hell. With Cortés presumed dead, Gonzalo de Salazar, an agent of the king, seized power in Mexico City. Salazar appropriated most of Cortés's property and had those men who remained loyal to him killed or imprisoned. The new leader ruled New Spain as a petty dictator, infuriating Spanish residents. Several Indian tribes, sensing a split among the Spaniards, rose up in rebellion. It seemed as if the whole fabric of New Spain was being torn apart.

As Cortés marched near the outskirts of Mexico City, Spanish townspeople greeted him as a hero who was so magnificent he had managed to cheat death. Even the Indians played fifes, beat on drums, and scattered flowers at his feet. In Mexico City, the residents seized Salazar and locked him in a cage, which they carried to the central plaza. There hundreds of New Spain's citizens stood in line to taunt and curse the man.

Cortés restored order in Mexico City, but waiting for him was a letter from King Charles. The king requested him to take the earliest possible ship to Spain. Cortés obeyed his monarch's order. In the spring of 1528 he set sail for the motherland of Spain, a country he had not seen for almost twenty-five years.

Cortés had left Spain a penniless young man; he returned traveling as a great lord. He carried so many goods to the motherland that he had to lease two ships for the voyage. For the amusement of his king and his countrymen, he transported Indian dancers,

Cortés's entry ino Toledo, Spain

jugglers, and acrobats. He also brought exotic-looking Indians—albinos with snow-white skin, dwarfs, and hunchbacks. In those days, Europeans derived great entertainment in gaping at unusual or freakish-looking people. To the wonderment of peasant farmers, Cortés also displayed caged birds and jaguars captured in the Mexican jungle.

Townspeople greeted Cortés in a manner rivaling the king himself. Not since Columbus had the Spaniards welcomed home an explorer so enthusiastically. Cortés had no idea how popular he had become with his countrymen. But Cortés's meeting with the Spanish king was a disappointment.

On the surface it seemed as if King Charles owed Cortés an enormous debt. His conquest of Mexico had made the Spanish Empire the largest in the world. Gold and silver mines in New Spain financed many of the king's projects, including the expansion of his war fleet. However, Cortés's many enemies had planted the seeds of mistrust in the mind of the Spanish king. Though Cortés had been for the most part a loyal subject, Charles feared he would someday betray the crown. The king allowed Cortés to expand his already enormous holdings in New Spain, but he refused to give the conquistador a high position in the colony's government.

A disappointed Cortés returned to New Spain in 1530. He settled in his palatial home in the town of Cuernavaca. Though he was refused a role in government, he enjoyed a steady stream of money from his wheat and cotton fields, his ranches, and his gold and silver mines. A lesser man would have retired into a life of luxury, but the rage to explore still burned in Cortés's heart.

Seeking new empires, he led a series of expeditions to the Pacific coast. He founded Acapulco, today Mexico's most celebrated resort city. Cortés used Acapulco as a shipbuilding center. Navigators on board his ships made the first accurate maps of Mexico's Pacific shoreline. Cortés led a mission into the Gulf of California, where he established an outpost at the present-day site of La Paz. His attempt to begin a colony there was a dismal failure, but today the waters of the Gulf of California are called the Sea of Cortés.

The shipbuilding and exploration ventures cost Cortés almost one million dollars in today's currency.

Scarlet macaw in Papagayo Park, Acapulco, Mexico

AQVAPOLQVE.

The expeditions earned nothing, and Cortés fell into debt. Nevertheless, he planned even more missions of discovery. He hoped to march north to the present-day American states of Arizona, New Mexico, and Texas. It was said that somewhere in those lands stood seven cities whose buildings were made of pure gold. Cortés was never able to search for those cities because he remained out of favor with government officials. Permission to explore the American Southwest was given to his rival conquistador, Francisco Vásquez de Coronado.

Seventeenth-century drawing of Acapulco, founded by Cortés

Charles, king of Spain and later Holy Roman Emperor

To meet the demands of his creditors, Cortés was forced to sell many of his Mexican land holdings. Despite the sales, his debts mounted. He believed the only solution to his financial troubles was to clear his name with the Spanish king and secure a government post in New Spain. Cortés sailed to Spain in 1540. He would never again return to the New World.

In Spain there seemed to be nothing Cortés could do to win the king's favor. He even participated in a disastrous Spanish military operation in North Africa, but Charles still refused to grant his wishes. Though he still owned vast estates in the New World, his money and his popularity in Spain dwindled. One

The castle of Cuesta near Seville,
Spain, where Cortés died in 1547

of his last letters to the king reads as if it were written by a common beggar rather than by the conqueror of Mexico:

"I thought that having labored in my earlier years I would enjoy rest in my old age. . . . I must return to my house [in New Spain]; I am no longer of an age to loiter at inns." But he ended the letter with a touch of his old Spanish pride: "It is better to lose one's wealth than one's soul."

On December 2, 1547, Cortés died in a small town near Seville. He was sixty-two years old. Though he was powerless and sickly, many of his countrymen mourned the death of Spain's greatest soldier.

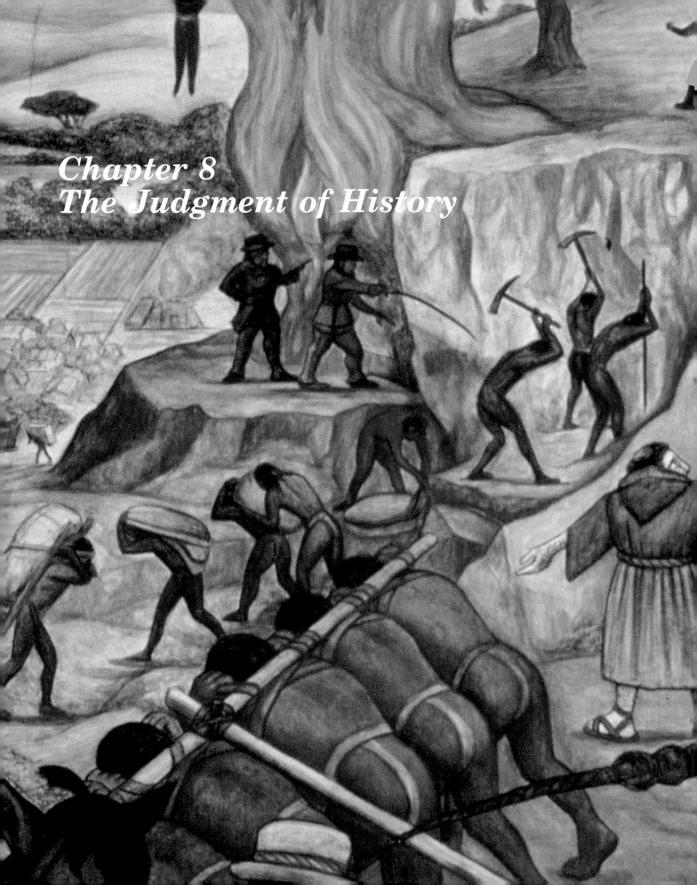

Chapter 8
The Judgment of History

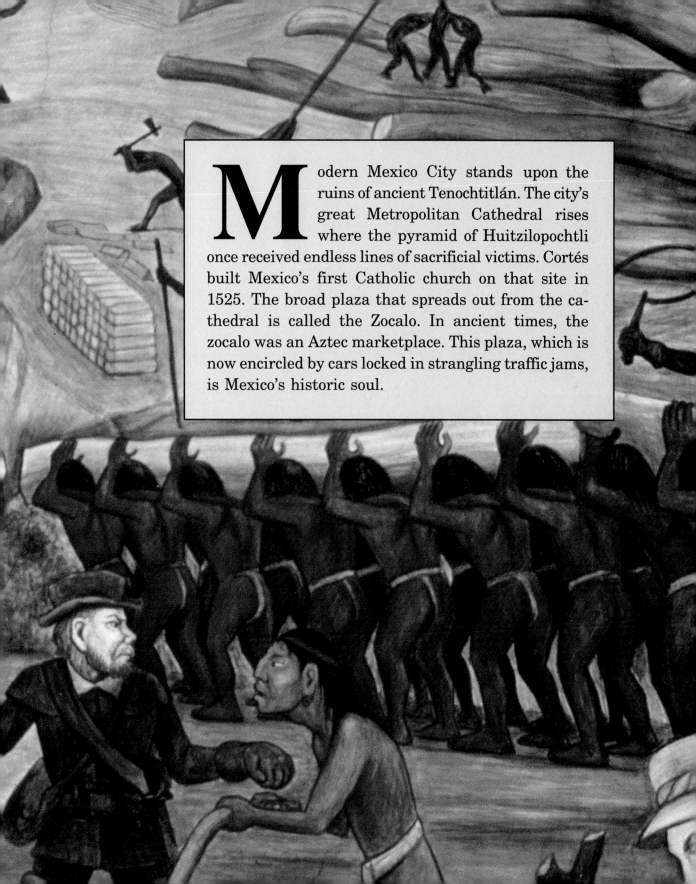

Modern Mexico City stands upon the ruins of ancient Tenochtitlán. The city's great Metropolitan Cathedral rises where the pyramid of Huitzilopochtli once received endless lines of sacrificial victims. Cortés built Mexico's first Catholic church on that site in 1525. The broad plaza that spreads out from the cathedral is called the Zocalo. In ancient times, the zocalo was an Aztec marketplace. This plaza, which is now encircled by cars locked in strangling traffic jams, is Mexico's historic soul.

Detail of Diego Rivera's mural "The Arrival of Cortés, 1519," in Mexico City's National Palace

On the east side of the Zocalo stands the huge National Palace, famed for the murals, or wall paintings, that adorn its hallways. The most celebrated of these murals were painted by the Mexican artist Diego Rivera, who died in 1957. Two side-by-side murals give Rivera's account of the Aztec conquest. In the left-hand mural, Rivera pictures the Aztecs, dressed in colorful costumes, peacefully going about their daily chores. The people are smiling, and one detail shows two small dogs romping playfully. Then Cortés arrives. In the right-hand mural, Spaniards are putting Aztecs in chains. One Spaniard brands an Aztec on the face with a red-hot iron. The same two dogs that were once lost in play are now shown snarling at each other fang to fang.

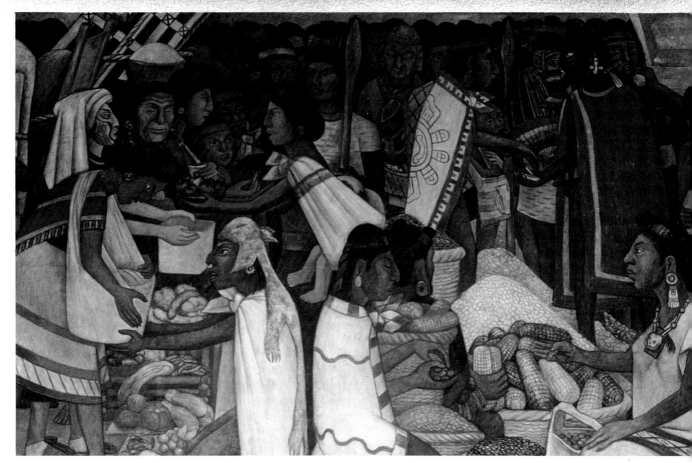

Diego Rivera's murals reflect an anti-Spanish view of history that is widespread in Mexico. After the conquest, Spain ruled Mexico for three hundred years. Though the country achieved much under Spain, many Mexicans look upon the Spanish era as a period of enslavement. Cortés is blamed for launching the reign of Spanish dominion.

Today it is impossible to find a public statue of Cortés anywhere in Mexico. One of the few places where his name is inscribed is on the wall of an ancient building in Mexico City called the Hospital de Jesus. Cortés founded a hospital on that site in 1528. He is buried below the present-day building. Even his burial site has had a tumultuous history, reflecting the nation's emotions toward the conqueror.

In 1566, almost twenty years after Cortés's death, a casket bearing his bones was dug from a Spanish grave and shipped to Mexico. There, according to his will, it was reburied near the grave of his mother, who had died while visiting New Spain. Twice Cortés's casket was shifted from spot to spot as New Spain officials built monuments to the colony's founder. Finally, in 1794, Cortés was laid to rest at the Hospital de Jesus.

But in the 1820s, after Mexico's War of Independence, anti-Spanish sentiment soared in the country.

Mexico's Church and Hospital de Jesus, founded by Cortés

Revolutionary leaders demanded that Cortés's bones be dug up and publicly burned. To protect the remains from mobs, priests dug up the casket and buried it in a "secret place." The burial site remained a mystery for more than a century. Then, in 1946, researchers discovered the casket under a remote corner of the Hospital de Jesus. The "secret place" turned out to be just a few feet from the old burial site. Cortés's bones are at rest now, but his image as a demon scourging the land remains alive in the minds and hearts of many Mexicans.

Cortés's coat of arms, inscribed with the motto "The judgment of God reached them, and his courage has strengthened my arm"

Does Cortés deserve his place as a villain in Mexican history? Cortés was a complex personality, and judging him is a complicated task. Certainly he should be looked upon in the light of his times. While conquering Mexico he tortured, enslaved, and executed Indians. But when doing these awful things, he was acting as any Spanish military leader would. In the Spanish army of his era, gentleness was considered to be a sign of weakness. Also, it must be remembered that Cortés lived during the Spanish Inquisition, when government and church leaders acted as if they were insensitive to the pain and suffering of others. At the height of Inquisition madness, men and women were burned at the stake in public squares amid an atmosphere not unlike that of a carnival.

Spanish Jews being put to death for their religious beliefs during the Spanish Inquisition

Yet Cortés often rose above the brutalities so common during his era. He sent letter after letter to the Spanish king, complaining about the abuses other Spaniards inflicted on the Indians. By the standards of later *conquistadores*, Cortés was almost merciful. Those who followed—Pizarro, Coronado, and others—seemed to delight in cruelty. Nor did Cortés possess the racism of many Spaniards, who regarded the dark-skinned Indians as less than human. To him, Indians were brothers with whites. He sincerely believed that, once they accepted Christianity, the Indians of Mexico would achieve greatness.

Spaniards forcing Indians to pan for gold in a stream

Popular Mexican history also brands Malinche as a traitor. Cortés and Malinche were close companions and eventually had a son—one of the first babies born of mixed Spanish and Mexican-Indian blood. As a skilled interpreter, Malinche was indispensable to Cortés's victory over the Aztecs. Today Malinche is regarded as a two-faced scoundrel who sold out her people to win the favor of the powerful conqueror. Her name invokes an often-used curse. If a boy favors American rock music over traditional Mexican rhythms, or if a girl prefers to wear jeans made in Europe, their friends will tell them, scornfully, "You are a malinche!"

Malinche, whom the Spaniards called Doña Marina; because of her role as Cortés's translator and spokesperson, she was called Malinche, meaning "tongue"

In the minds of many Mexicans, the greatest hero of the conquest story is Cuauhtémoc, the last Aztec king. He rallied his people to fight for every inch of the ancient capital's grounds. He endured Cortés's torture manfully and died defying the conquistador. It is widely believed in Mexico that Cuauhtémoc recovered the treasure lost in Lake Texcoco and took the secret of its whereabouts to his grave.

Above Mexico City's busiest boulevard, Paseo de la Reforma, stands a statue of Cuauhtémoc poised to hurl a spear. Each year on the anniversary of his torture, dancers costumed like ancient Aztecs perform around the statue's base.

Statue of Cuauhtémoc

Still, Malinche and Cuauhtémoc are supporting players in the drama of the conquest. The leading character is the man from the windswept province of Extremadura in Spain.

Even his severest critics in Mexico recognize Cortés's many accomplishments. He was a fearless explorer and one of history's most successful military commanders. No single individual did more to mold Mexico after the conquest than did Cortés. He gave the country Christianity and the Spanish language. Even more important, he made possible a migration that created a new race of men and women. After the conquest, Mexico became a land of three races—the Indians, the whites, and the mestizos, who were of mixed Indian and white bloodlines. At first the new race was a tiny minority, but it was destined for greatness.

Today the vast majority of Mexicans are mestizos. They are *La Raza*, the Race, the people of modern Mexico.

In today's Mexico, Columbus Day is called *Dia de la Raza*, Day of the Race. It is a joyous holiday that features schoolchildren parading in town squares. During the celebrations, Mexicans praise the Italian sea captain as the creator of the mestizo race. But Columbus never set foot on Mexican soil.

Dia de la Raza might well be held on the day Cortés landed in Mexico, though few Mexicans would suggest such a change. In Mexico, Cortés will probably never shed his image as a cruel, greedy conquistador.

Cortés is honored, indirectly, on a plaque that hangs near the Zocalo in Mexico City. The plaque marks the site of a furious battle between Aztecs and Spaniards.

It does not mention Cortés by name, but says about the climactic war he waged: "It was neither triumph nor defeat—it was instead the painful birth of the mestizo people who are Mexico today."

Painting of a conquistador and an Aztec "eagle" warrior

Capitullo Lxxvi de como

El marques boluio de tlaxcala A tez
cuco. y alli hiço. los vergantines y de alli
Vino. a mexico. y de como el rrey quauhte
moc se defendio y mantubo contra el
valerossa mente

Viendo. quauhtemoc y sabiendo por sus es
pias y mensajeros. por momentos la determina
çion delos españoles, (enlo qual estauatan
çircunspeto y vigilante. que no se descuidaua
nada). y que ya se determinacian. de boluer
A mexico. no solo incitaua. Alas nasçiones y
pia. socorro para junta mente. Sacian el y los
dela çiudad. grandes saçrifiçios y oraçiones
a sus dioses. y les ofreçian grandes. saçrifi
çios pidiendoles. fauor y victoria contra los es
pañoles y contra los demas. sus enemigos, pero
ya sera. por demas. por que aun rrepuestos de

ninguno, llorauan. amarga mente pero contodo
esso estauan en sus trece. de morir. o defender
su çiudad, y esto tienen. los indios que si propo
nen de haçer vna cossa y en pica a menospre
çiar. la vida y a tenella. en poco n stemi. in
Deue hasta morir. o ssalir. consu interes. lo
lo lleuan. adelante qual quier mal propesi
to. o rranca, y si para esto es menester pieuan
ça façil cossa sera prouallo. por que en essas au
Diençias vemos y los que conellos tratamos
vemos cada dia, que si vn pueblo, contra
otro. leuantan. algun. Pleyto. o quistion se
las estançias contra. la caueçera. o los mate
guales. o bassallos, contra. susseñor hasta la
muerte. Seperssiguen. o hasta. salir. conla
ya porcossa. muy injusta que sea, y contra
rraçon, por ser gente. muy caueçida, virtu
sial, sobre lo qual. mitienen respecto apa
mihermano. mi pariente ni amigo. mientra
el tiempo que le tura. el interes nasçe

Appendices

Sources of Information about Cortés

We know about Cortés's activities in the New World from several sources. One is the *Historia verdadera* of Bernal Díaz del Castillo, one of Cortés's soldiers. A second is the *Historia de la Conquista*, by Francisco López de Gómara. Since he was Cortés's personal secretary, López de Gómara sometimes tended to make Cortés's deeds sound more glorious than they were. Cortés himself wrote of his adventures in his *Despatches*. Fray Diego Durán was another historian of the Aztec conquest. The page at left comes from his *Story of the Aztec Indians in South America*.

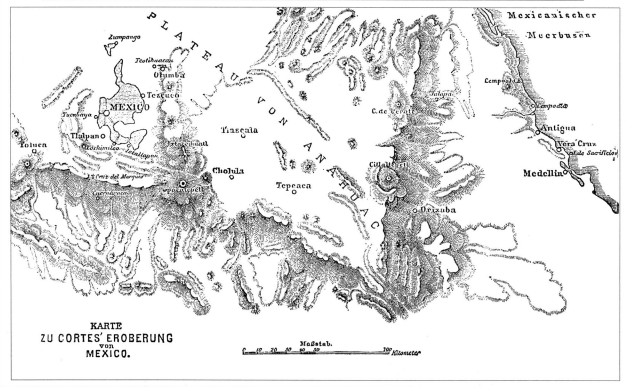

KARTE
ZU CORTES' EROBERUNG
von
MEXICO.

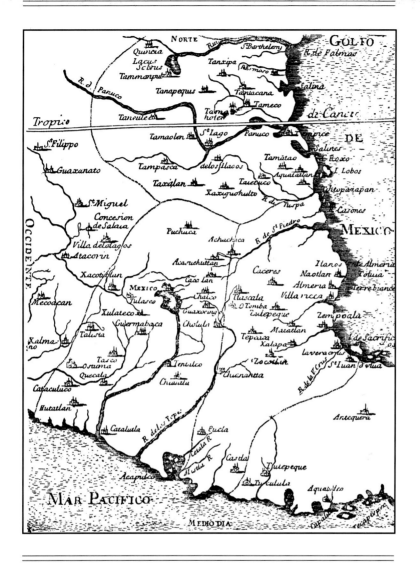

After Cortés's conquest, historians and mapmakers of many nations tried to illustrate the lands he visited. The top map on the opposite page first appeared in 1580 in a book by the Italian historian Clavigero. It is one of many attempts to depict Lake Texcoco, the island city, and surrounding areas. Beneath it is a German map showing the area of Cortés's marches. The more recent map above, by the Spanish historian Herrera, is a more accurate version of the area.

Timeline of Events in Cortés's Lifetime

1485—Hernando Cortés is born in Spain's Extremadura province

1488—Portuguese explorer Bartholomeu Dias sails around the Cape of Good Hope, Africa's southern tip

1492—Spanish forces capture the Moors' stronghold at Granada; commissioned by Ferdinand and Isabella of Spain, Christopher Columbus arrives in the New World

1497—John Cabot discovers the North American continent, probably at Labrador

1499—Cortés enters the university at Salamanca

1500—Pedro Cabral reaches the coast of Brazil and claims it for Portugal; the Amazon River is discovered

1502—Christopher Columbus explores the coast of present-day Panama on his fourth voyage

1503—Spain begins slave trade in the New World

1504—At the age of nineteen, Cortés first sails for the New World

1510—Spanish explorer Vasco Núñez de Balboa arrives in present-day Panama

1511—Cortés arrives on the island of Cuba as secretary to Diego Velázquez and settles down as a rancher

1519—Cortés and his soldiers sail to the Yucatán Peninsula and march inland to Tenochtitlán; Ferdinand Magellan begins his voyage to circumnavigate the globe

1520—Aztecs force the Spaniards out of Tenochtitlán

1521—Cortés conquers the Aztecs, beginning three centuries of Spanish domination in Central America

1524—Cortés marches to Honduras

1528—Cortés founds a hospital in Mexico City on the site of the present-day Hospital de Jesus; he sails back to Spain at the request of King Charles

1530—Cortés returns to New Spain, settling in his home in Cuernavaca, Mexico

1535—Cortés travels to what is now Baja California

1540—Deep in debt, Cortés returns to Spain for the last time

1547—Cortés dies in a small town near Seville, Spain

Glossary of Terms

albino—A person or animal lacking pigmentation, or coloring; albinos usually have white skin and hair and pink or blue eyes

astrologer—One who studies stars and other heavenly bodies to explain things that happen in people's lives

astronomer—One who makes scientific studies of stars and other heavenly bodies

barbarian—A crude, uncultured, or uncivilized person

barricaded—Blocked off; behind a barrier

booty—Goods taken in wartime from conquered people

breach—A gap; a broken or torn condition

brigantine—A small, two-masted ship

brutalities—Cruel, severe actions

cacique—Term for an Indian chief, used especially in areas explored by Spaniards

calamity—A disaster or misfortune

causeway—A bridge; a raised roadway over water

conquistador—A Spanish leader in the conquest of Central and South America

controversial—Giving rise to disputes between differing views

cypress—A type of evergreen tree

emissary—Someone sent as a representative or spokesperson for another

encomiendo—A huge tract of land, plus the Indians who lived on it, awarded to a Spanish settler in the New World

epidemic—A widespread outbreak of a disease

figurine—A small statue

freebooter—A person who goes on a military or exploring expedition to gain treasure or other material prizes

friar—A male member of a religious order who teaches and preaches and does not own personal property

gruesome—Horrible, disgusting, or distasteful

idol—A statue or picture that is worshiped as a god

inkling—A hint, clue, or notion

lieutenant—A military officer's rank; an aide who represents or acts for another person

litter—A stretcher or bed equipped with poles for carrying a sick or injured person

luster—A shiny glow

massacre—The cruel killing of a large number of people

mercenary—A hired fighter who serves mainly for money, rather than out of patriotism

mestizo—A person of mixed blood

metropolis—A large city

mutiny—To rebel or to resist authority

nomadic—Having no fixed home; wandering from place to place

ordeal—An extremely difficult experience

palatial—Like a palace

pantheon—The collection of all the official gods of a group of people

plaque—A wooden or metal sign commemorating a person or event

plunderer—One who takes goods from conquered peoples

pyramid—A structure that usually has triangular sides and rises to a point at the top

ragtag—Dressed in rags; messy

ravaged—Violently destroyed

raze—To destroy to the ground

ritual—A ceremony with a set series of actions

rout—A defeat marked by disorder and confusion

shambles—A wreck; a mess

sophisticated—Highly developed or having broad experience

tortilla—A thin bread made from the flour of cornmeal or wheat

torture—To cruelly inflict pain

treachery—Betrayal of someone's trust

tumultuous—Disorderly; violently confused

veteran—A soldier who has served for a long time

Bibliography

For further reading, see:

Cortés, Hernando. *Letters from Mexico*. Translated by A.R. Pagden. New York: Grossman Publishers, 1971.

Díaz del Castillo, Bernal. *The Discovery and Conquest of Mexico*. Translated by A.P. Maudslay. New York: Farrar, Straus, and Cudahy, 1956.

Fehrenbach, T.R. *Fire and Blood (A History of Mexico)*. New York: Collier Books, 1979.

Gómara, Francisco López de. *Cortés, the Life of the Conqueror*. Translated by Lesley Byrd Simpson. Los Angeles: University of California Press, 1964.

Innes, Hammond. *The Conquistadors*. New York: Alfred A. Knopf, 1969.

Johnson, William Weber. *Cortés (Conquering the New World)*. New York: Paragon House, 1987.

Kandell, Jonathan. *La Capital (The Biography of Mexico City)*. New York: Random House, 1988.

Parkes, Henry Bamford. *A History of Mexico*. Boston: Houghton Mifflin Company, 1969.

Index

Page numbers in boldface type indicate illustrations.

Picture Identifications for Chapter Opening Spreads

6-7—The Central Valley of Mexico near Mexico City
10-11—Columbus's ships on his first voyage to the Americas
24-25—Carvings of skulls on an Aztec altar dedicated to the sun
32-33—A rain forest near Palenque in southern Mexico
46-47—The Aztec capital of Tenochtitlán
66-67—Detail of an Aztec warrior stone
82-83—Shells on the beach at Cozumel, off the Mexican coast
102-103—Mural by Diego Rivera at Mexico's National Palace:
    "The Arrival of Cortes, 1519"

Picture Acknowledgments

The Bettmann Archive: 9, 23, 41, 51, 81, 95, 108

© Virginia Grimes: 82-83

Historical Pictures Service, Chicago: 2, 19, 28 (top), 31, 35, 38, 39, 42, 45, 58, 69, 71, 75, 77, 89, 99, 100

North Wind Picture Archives: 13, 15, 18, 28 (bottom), 29, 30, 52, 53, 55, 59, 61, 62, 63 (top), 64, 65, 70, 72, 73, 76, 79, 85, 86, 92, 93, 97, 101, 106, 107, 109, 110, 116 (2 pictures), 117

Odyssey/Frerck/Chicago— © Robert Frerck: 6-7, 12 (top), 16, 21 (top), 26, 32-33, 84, 88, 113; Museum of Mexico City, 5; by Rafael Monleon, Naval Museum, Madrid, 10-11; National Museum of Anthropology, Mexico City, Mexico, 8, 24-25, 27, 46-47, 54, 63 (bottom), 66-67; Diego Rivera, National Palace, Mexico City, 36, 87, 102-103, 104, 105

Chip and Rosa Maria de la Cueva Peterson: 50, 111

Photri: 12 (bottom), 49, 114

© Bob and Ira Spring: 20, 21 (bottom)

SuperStock International, Inc.: 4; © Karl Kummels, 43

Valan: © V. Wilkinson: 91, 94; © Kennon Cooke, 98

Cover illustration by Steven Gaston Dobson

About the Author

R. Conrad Stein was born and grew up in Chicago. He attended the University of Illinois, where he earned a degree in history. He is the author of many books, articles, and short stories written for young readers. Mr. Stein now lives in Chicago with his wife and their daughter, Janna. Mexico is Mr. Stein's second home. He lived almost ten years in San Miguel de Allende, a village north of Mexico City. The Stein family still spends summers in San Miguel. Mexican history has always fascinated Mr. Stein, and he has read many books on the subject. He was delighted to write this book on Cortés and the Aztec conquest.